S0-ATD-900

267.182
Si 12

THE WORD MADE FLESH

The Chicago Catholic Worker and the Emergence of Lay Activism in the Church

Francis J. Sicius

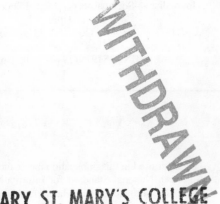

LIBRARY ST. MARY'S COLLEGE

184892

UNIVERSITY
PRESS OF
AMERICA

Lanham • New York • London

Copyright © 1990 by
University Press of America®, Inc.
4720 Boston Way
Lanham, Maryland 20706

3 Henrietta Street
London WC2E 8LU England

All rights reserved
Printed in the United States of America
British Cataloging in Publication Information Available

Library of Congress Cataloging-in-Publication Data

Sicius, Francis J.
The word made flesh : the "Chicago Catholic worker" and the emergence
of lay activism in the church / Francis J. Sicius.
p.   cm.
Includes bibliographical references.
1. Chicago Catholic worker (1938).
2. Journalism, Religious—United States—History—20th century.
3. Catholic Church—United States—History—20th century.
4. Laity—Catholic Church—History—20th century.
5. Church and social problems—United States—History—20th century.
6. Journalism—Social aspects—United States—20th century.
I. Title.
PN4899.C4C387   1990   267'.18277311—dc20   90–33438 CIP

ISBN 0–8191–7794-6 (alk. paper)

$31.83 MW 7-24-91 (W.a.)

™ The paper used in this publication meets the minimum requirements of
American National Standard for Information Sciences—Permanence
of Paper for Printed Library Materials, ANSI Z39.48–1984.

This work is dedicated to the memory of my mother: Elizabeth Jane Sicius

ACKNOWLEDGMENTS

This work has been with me for quite a few years and therefore has had time to acquire a number of personal debts. The earliest goes to my friend William Miller who first introduced me to the Worker movement. He also, through his example, awoke in me the love for teaching and writing which has become my career. As I read the scholarly literature on the Catholic Worker, I noticed that few have ignored this thoughtful man's intellectual contribution to an understanding of the movement. Now I am pleased to join the company of those who have written accolades to his efforts. Another important debt is owed to my graduate advisor James Penick who fifteen years ago took me through the early drafts of this work. It was his good humor, and excellent scholarship which helped turn this manuscript from simply a product of enthusiasm to one of serious thought. There are a number of other intellectual debts which ought to be acknowledged, but the most recent, and at the moment, the one that looms largest in my mind, is that owed to Notre Dame editor An Rice. Although unable to publish the work through her press, she gave me advise and encouragement to continue working on it. This motivation, along with her detailed reading and critique, is the most important reason why this work is not now sitting on a shelf as an unpublished manuscript.

I also would like to thank all those connected with the Chicago Catholic Worker who shared their homes, their hospitality and their thoughts with me. Without them this work would would have been impossible. I am particularly grateful to Jim O'Gara who opened up the files of *Commonweal* for me, and to Ed Marciniak and Arthur Falls who allowed me to read through those parts of their personal files which were relevant to the history I was researching. These men had the keen sense to know that not only were they about important work but what they did should be preserved for posterity. I must also thank my favorite librarian, Margaret Elliston, who through her able direction of computer search material and interlibrary loans, turned our small college library into a good research center. Finally, a special thanks to my friend Ted Senna who helped me through the programming mysteries of a laser printer. Although there was much help in doing this work, I am sure many errors remain, and for these I take the responsibility, for if those people whom I have mentioned here were able to sit down and collectively do this work it would have been error free.

CONTENTS

Acknowledgments.............................v

Preface....................................ix

I.   Peter Maurin and the Catholic Worker........1

II.   The Chicago Beginning....................21

III.   Charity.................................41

IV.   Racial Harmony..........................53

V.   Anti-Semitism...........................65

VI.   Labor..................................79

VII.   Industrial Unionism.....................95

VIII.   Pacifism...............................109

IX.   Alternatives to War....................127

X.   Work...................................143

XI.   The Post War Years.....................153

XII.   The Word Made Flesh....................171

Bibliography.................................179

Index..193

PREFACE

In Vienna as elsewhere, May first was a worker's holiday. But on this day in 1933 the Ringstrasse remained virtually abandoned. The cafes were empty, and the gardens were silent. Barbed wire and armed police blighted the fragile elegance of the traditional gathering place, as fear interrupted customary rituals. In New York, fear also reigned. Police Commissioner James Bolan cancelled all furloughs for the city's 19,000 police officers and stationed 2,000 of them with machine guns around Union Square where he expected 50,000 demonstrators that afternoon.

The great world depression was in its third year, and as it continued to widen the chasm between rich and poor, it provoked memories of the violent eruptions of the 1870s and eighties. Some thrived on the tension. Addressing a May Day rally in Berlin, Adolph Hitler evoked the image of the ancient Teutonic warrior. He urged the "folk" of Germany to recapture that medieval spirit and rise up against the economic oppression of foreignors. Others anguished over the emerging rage. From a prison in Yerovda, India, Mahatma Ghandi announced that he would begin a fast in order to purify his soul and to remind the world that oppression would not be ended by terrorism. When asked why he felt the need for another fast, Ghandi confessed that a tension had been raging within him for days.[1]

The depression had gone on for another bitter year, and an increase in memberships in both extreme left and right wing political groups seemed to be a sign that the frustration of the poor would soon explode into raw violence. May Day promised to provide the spark for the human powder keg, but for a few exceptions, the day passed tranquilly. The biggest surprise to police officers of New York occurred when Com-

---

[1]*New York Times*, May 1, 1933.

munists and Socialist Worker Party members, despite their sworn enmity toward each other-pledged alliance against their new common foe, the fascists. The unexpectedly peaceful day served as the setting for the birth of a new radical movement.

Despite the ban on subversive material issued by the police , a small group of enthusiasts distributed a new journal that day entitled *The Catholic Worker.* To many of those who saw the newspaper, such a title must have seemed oxymoronic, for if there ever was a power that buttressed the status quo of wealth and authority it was the Catholic Church. But the new periodical was addressed to those ". . .sitting on benches, huddling in shelters, [and] walking the streets". It explained that the Catholic Church had a humane alternative to the oppressive nature of industrial capitalism and stood with those victimized by that system.

The Catholics who distributed the paper that May Day in 1933 created a significant date in the history of Catholicism in the United States. For it marked the first time that a group of American Catholics proposed their faith as a basis for radical political activism. Over the course of the next five decades, the *Catholic Worker* message which began on the street corners of New York eventually found its way into episcopal letters. But in 1933 the appearance on the street corner was enough for history to absorb. Ever since John Carroll became the first American bishop in 1789, American Catholic leaders and writers have attempted to defend their coreligionists by asserting that the basic elements of Catholicism and Americanism were compatible. In the mid-nineteenth century Isaac Hecker went so far as to suggest that Catholicism created an intellectual and spiritual environment in which democracy could thrive.

With its bold message the *Catholic Worker* turned the Church in the opposite direction. Quoting authorities no less significant than the Pope himself, they attacked a fundamental premise of American democracy, liberal capitalism. From its inception, the *Catholic Worker* became the intellectual focal point for the Catholic left in this country. The fact that such a movement had to be created by an immigrant to America, Peter Maurin, and a convert to the faith, Dorothy Day, was a symptom of the history of the American Catholic Church up to that time. But the movement's peculiar combination of Catholic thought and social activism touched the nascent spirit of a new generation in the Church, and soon legions of believers in this fresh view of theology emerged across the nation. In Chicago, an early leader in the civil rights movement wrote of the Catholic Worker, "Finally someone is enlisting the Catholic Church on my side, where I believe it should have been all along."[2]Dwight Mc Donald of the *New Yorker* magazine pointed out that "a curious paradox was involved in the rise of the Catholic Worker movement. Historically," he noted, the church had been restricted primarily to the lower classes. By the thirties however, "Catholic immigrants were sending their children and grandchildren to college and Catholics began producing middle class intellectuals as full of reforming zeal as their Protestant counterparts."[3] Although the journalist's comments create an historic picture which the progeny of old American Catholic families such as the Barry's and Carroll's would deny, the generalization is valid for the immigrant church rooted in the turn of the century. And as historian David O'Brien has pointed out, the children of that generation of Catholics who reached maturity in

---

[2]Interview with Arthur Falls, founder of the Chicago Catholic Worker movement, June 19, 1976, Western Springs, Illinois.

[3]Dwight Mc Donald, Foolish Things of the World", *New Yorker* (October 11, 1951), 37. See also Francis Lally, *The Catholic Church in a Changing America* (Boston:Little Brown and Company, 1962), 48.

the depression years were not content to merely follow clerical leadership. They sought a more vital church which would actively participate in the reconstruction of the social, political, and economic structure of the country. This new generation found the promise for such a church in the pages of the *Catholic Worker*. The enthusiasm created by the publication of this paper caused the formation of "study clubs" across the nation and eventually the establishment of Catholic Worker houses and farms.

One such group emerged in Chicago, and prior to the war it represented one of the most significant branches of the Catholic Worker family. Before the war wielded its divisive force, the Chicago group opened a number of houses of hospitality, organized a farm commune experiment, pioneered in race relations within the city and the Church, and published a newspaper.

There are two histories of the Catholic Worker. One is the movement itself, complete with heroes, heroines and hundreds of interesting vignettes. Judged in this context, or rather solely in the context of recent American history, the movement becomes one more social protest in a period overburdened with them. The other story of the Catholic Worker however, places it within the scope of the history of the Church, and in this context it becomes very significant. It shows how the Catholic Church has survived for centuries, because the ideas developed by people associated with this movement gave the Catholic Church in America a new energy and spirit at a time when it threatened to disintegrate before the economic and political challenges of industrialism and nationalism.

When issues on social, economic and liturgical reform first appeared in the pages of the *Catholic Worker*, they were called outlandish by a majority of the clergy and hierarchy, but within thirty years these same ideas became the focal point of several papers published by the U.S. Bishops' Conference. In the 1930's Dorothy Day was criticized by the hierarchy for her radicalism, but in 1975 she addressed the the College of Cardinal's World Conference in Philadelphia. These examples mark the development not only of the Catholic Worker but also of the entire American Catholic Church when it shed its image of obedient servant to the universal Catholic Church and became one of the leading forces in a revitalized Church which demanded participation in rectifying the injustices of modern political economic systems. As the Church increasingly confronts the kingdoms of Adam Smith and Karl Marx, the ideas of the Catholic Worker become more prophetic. For this group of young Catholics in the 1930's rediscovered within the old theology of their Church a new synthesis with which they set out to build, as Peter Maurin said, "the new within the shell of the old".

Although many would enter then leave the Catholic Worker, few remained unaffected by what they learned there. Nowhere is this continuity and consistency of thought more clearly demonstrated than in the story of those who founded the movement in Chicago. Many who reached intellectual maturity while members of this group had in later life a profound effect on American Catholicism. Among its members were John Cogley, who edited the *Commonweal* magazine while it was becoming the leading layman's Catholic journal in the country, James O'Gara, another former editor of *Commonweal*, and Ed Marciniak a leader in Catholic Social Action in Chicago for over fifty years. Added to these few are the scores of others who started Catholic Worker farming communes or who revitalized old parishes with their idealism.

The Catholic Worker movement still exists in Chicago as elsewhere. Today however, it is very different. It has become as much a shrine as a forum. No longer is the world full of energetic idealists eager to change it. For better or worse, the decade of the thirties with its earnest crusades is over. Students, scholars and workers still mingle at the Worker houses. Some are there, as always, for the free soup, or a bed; but others seek a more illusive sustenance, the spirit and idealism which motivated an earlier generation. The comparison however is not a fair one. The world on the horizon which Peter Maurin feared has arrived. Bourgeois dreams have encompassed the spiritual idealism of previous generations. Sense has superceded soul and material obligations have taken precedence over responsibility to family and community.

The Catholic Workers of the thirties operated within the context of a different spiritual and intellectual universe. They struggled against the fragmenting force of industrialization and the false community of the nation and groped for change in the direction of harmony and universality. The result of this struggle was a new application of a very old theology. As one former Catholic Worker recalled, "It seems long ago and far away. We had a great deal of confidence we could change the world. the world has changed but not as we anticipated.[4] In those early days of the movement when hope remained stronger, the Catholic Worker provided and ambience in which ideals flourished. As Ed Marciniak stated and others would concur, "The first outlines of my desires and aspirations for my manhood came to me during my early days with the Catholic Worker".[5]

Francis J. Sicius
St. Thomas University
Miami, Florida

---

[4]Catherine Reser to author, April 22, 1976.

[5]Undated, unaddressed letter in Marciniak papers, file: "early forties".

CHAPTER I

PETER MAURIN AND THE CATHOLIC WORKER

In early June 1936, Peter Maurin left the Catholic Worker house in New York and visited the parks, tenderloin areas and parishes of Chicago.[1] He was a scholar, and although the editor of *America*, Wilfrid Parsons, called him the most well-read man he had ever known, Maurin preferred the spoken word to the written. Consequently he often traveled the country teaching, sometimes preaching, his views on religion, politics and the economy.

In Chicago, as elsewhere, most people ignored this bespectacled, bedraggled man with the heavy French accent, and as he lectured from crumpled notes which he pulled out of one of his pockets, they usually walked by. But some listened to the apparently bleak vagabond, and what they heard were ideas which provided the roots for an intellectual upheaval within the American Catholic Church.

The Jesuit priests from St. Ignatius on the North Side were interested in what Maurin had to say and one evening they invited him to speak to their parishoners. As he stood in the parish hall of the Church, which boasted a beautiful cupola, he reminded his listeners that "we need parish homes as well as parish domes".[2] His hosts invited him to spend the night, and after a good rest in a suite reserved for visiting dignitaries, he travelled downtown to Lower Wacker

---

[1] Account of Maurin's trip to Chicago in June, 1936 is based on an interview with Msgr. John Hayes, June 14, 1976, Chicago, Illinois.

[2] Peter Maurin, *The Green Revolution* (Chicago: Franciscan Herald Press, 1977) 6.

Drive, a thoroughfare which ran under Chicago's "Loop". During the depression years this underground roadway served as a "hotel" for hundreds of homeless trying to shelter themselves from the harsh winds which blew in off Lake Michigan. "Although you may be called bums and panhandlers" he probably told the men gathered there, "you are in fact ambassadors of God."[3] His hosts that night also offered him the best accomodations they could offer: a section of walkway near a burning trashcan, and Maurin accepted it as graciously as he had accepted the facilities of the night before.

During his time in Chicago Maurin spoke whereever he could. Neither political dispostion nor economic circumstance mattered. Whether on a street corner or Rotarian luncheon, if he had an audience, he spoke. If passersby ignored him he might push a copy of the *Catholic Worker* into their hands for consideration when they had more time to think. So clear was Maurin's message in his own mind, he felt only a little reflection was necessary for anyone to grasp it. Maurin had a successful visit to Chicago that summer, for out of it came the formation of the first Catholic Worker group in that city.

Although he was not totally in accord with this movement which he helped found in New York, it was the one group which most closely elicited his views of church and society. Maurin had to accomodate himself to the Worker movement because his view of Catholicism differed greatly from that of most of his fellow believers in America.

Maurin, a Frenchman, had a vision of the Church that was quite unfamiliar to Americans in the 1930's. Born in Europe in 1877, he had as a young student come under the influence of Pope Leo XIII and his efforts to reconcile Catholicism with the modern world. Leo opened the Vatican archives and enlisted an army of scholars to help breathe a new spirit into a generation mesmerized by the promise of unlimited material growth and

---

[3]Ibid, 4.

scientific development. This papal crusade left
a legacy which still influences political thought
in Europe.[4]
   Maurin's writing reveals the influence of
this renaissance of Catholic thought. It also
reflects the entire panorama of social criticism
which proliferated in nineteenth century Europe.
The social critics of the nineteenth century
varied greatly in their perspectives and although
they included Catholic traditionalists, as well
as socialists and anarchists they shared certain
themes. They all condemned the fragmentation
produced by competitive industrial capitalism,
and they sought a new synthesis which would take
advantage of the progress of the nineteenth
century in a more humanizing manner.
   In the nineteenth century United States,
such a spectrum of social thought hardly existed.
Although most Americans shared the reformist zeal
of their European cousins, most of their energy
was sapped by the anti-slavery campaign and the
war which followed it. Following that crusade,
the final expansion of the frontier and the second industrial revolution held such great promise of material growth that there was little need
or tolerance for social criticism. Consequently,
in the 1930's when the Great Depression closed
the door on expansion and material progress ,
Americans lacked an intellectual tradition which
could provide meaningful reflection on the
calamity. Those who were puzzled over the collapse of the economy and the loss of their jobs
had to derive answers from the loudest voices
echoing from Europe. And in the thirties, quasi-
fascists and communists who scrawled economic
programs on makeshift banners provided most of
the intellectual fodder for those trying to make
some sense of the decade's distortions.
   Maurin, who travelled throughout America as
a worker and observer in the twenties and early

----

   [4]Carlton Hayes, *A Generation of Materialism,
1871-1900* (New York: Harper and Row, 1941), pp.
141-145.

thirties, knew there was more to the economic and social problems than slogans could cure. He had a clear idea of what caused the Depression and also how to end it. Put simply, he believed the problem arose from the excesses of corporate capitalism and the solution lay in the economic theories contained in Catholic theology. Maurin's view was not original, but his attempt to introduce it to secular America was. In this country, which by law remains religiously neutral, the mixture of politics and religion seemed a dangerous and peculiar aberration.

Maurin was unaffected by this nuance in the American political tradition and he carried his message wherever he could and talked with whomever would listen. He attempted to lighten the complexity of his synthesis by lecturing in blank verse . Whenever a crowd of one or twenty would gather around him he would begin his instruction. His own explanation of the stock market crash seemed trite when delivered in his curious style, but he made precisely the same point that many economic historians have made since:

After the World War
people tried to believe
that a new era
had dawned upon the world.
People thought
that they had found a solution
to the problem of
mass distribution.
People thought
that the time had come
of a two car garage,
and a chicken in every pot
and a sign "To Let"
on front of every poorhouse.
And everyone wanted to cash in
on the future prosperity.
So the stock promoters got busy
and stocked people with stock

til they got stuck.[5]

Maurin presented in his so-called "Easy Essays" an historic outline that traced the decline of a philosophic tradition which had humanized the economic process. By the nineteenth century, economic philosophy had become so devoid of morality, that Karl Marx could separate economic history from social, cultural, political and religious history. Marx built his philosophy on the intellectual foundations of the enlightenment which had dethroned religion, and into this vacuum he placed the economic fact.

Maurin remained unimpressed with this nineteenth century transvaluation. To him, that which humanized should remain central to any philosophic synthesis. And despite its faults, the Church remained the focal point of the Western humanistic tradition. Maurin was not alone in his views. In England for example, a generation prior to Maurin, John Henry Newman came to similar conclusions when he abandoned the Church of England for Rome.

Maurin's vision stood counter to the dominant intellectual view which measured Western progress from the end of the middle ages. To Maurin, the middle ages which was dominated by the idea of the "Common Good", represented the apex of human economic thought. Since the thirteenth century, Maurin believed that economic thought had devolved to a system based totally on profit in which people were no longer interested in

> . . .selling useful goods
> but in making money
> on any kind of goods. . .
> and the producer
> ceased to think in terms of service
> and began to think

---

[5]Peter Maurin, *The Green Revolution: Easy Essays on Catholic Radicalism*(Chicago: Omega Graphics, 1976), p.106.

in terms of profits.

The harmonic and humanizing force of the Church which had guided economic philosophy through the middle ages had been neutralized in the sixteenth century when

John Calvin decided
to legalize
money lending at interest
in spite of the teachings
of the prophets of Israel
and the Fathers of the Church.

Maurin wrote that by the time the Industrial Revolution arrived and transformed economic life in Europe, Western philosophy had abandoned its heritage by severing all connectios between moral obligation and economic activity.

These were not Maurin's conclusions alone. Nineteenth century intellectual history provides a panorama of works condemning the spiritual emptiness of the age. At one extreme was Marx, the anti-religionist who tried to provide a resolution to the spiritual alienation of the working class, and at the other end of the spectrum was Dostoevsky, the Russian Orthodox, who in the *Brothers Karamazov*, has Ivan ask "why your Jesuits and Inqusitors have united simply for vile material gain? Whay can't there be among them one martyr oppressed by great sorrow and loving humanity?"

Little occurred in the nineteenth century to change the conditions that many censured, but Maurin lived in the twentieth century. He, as others did, thought he was witnessing the decline of capitalism. The stock market had crashed, businesses were failing and neither Wall Street nor Washington seemed to have any solutions. On the streets there were enough disillusioned people to compel would-be reformers to believe that the time was right to present a different order to things.

The ambience of the thirties stimulated Maurin. He began to distribute and to preach his

6

economic plan, in Union Square, at a rotary club meeting, in a park, or in a university faculty lounge, wherever there might be an interested audience he would go. He hoped to find a partner for his one-man revolution, and that person would find another and eventually they would , as he used to say, "build the new within the shell of the old".

Of course in the objective view of things, Maurin failed. He did not rally a mass movement to his cause, no legislation was passed at his suggestion and even in the intellectual world, he has caused barely a ripple in the sea of scholarship. However ideas need not be measured by objective scales. Intellectual historians ought to use different criteria. They cannot simply ask "How many?" but "Who?"; and they cannot merely quantify results, but must also ask "To what end?". And the answer to these questions is that Peter Maurin affected the people necessary to bring a much needed fresh breath of spirit to American Catholicism.

The outline of Maurin's plan appeared in his "Easy Essays which was the title under which his free verse appeared in the *Catholic Worker*. These columns provided catch phrases for those attracted by simple explanations, but for the more perspicacious, Maurin included sources which provided complete bibliography of nineteenth and early twentieth century social thought. Frequently his essays began a verse with "According to R.H. Tawney. . ." or "Kropotkin says. . ." or "Emmanuel Mounier wrote a book called the *Personalist Manifesto* . . . ." Another essay began "If you want to know. . . read. . " and it listed books ranging from Alexis Carrel's book on industrialism to Jacques Maritain's *Freedom in the Modern World*. His reading lists placed particular emphasis on Catholic thinkers and taken together, this substantial bibliography provided the intellectual foundation for his plan of voluntary socialism based on principles of Christian personalism and communal responsibility.

7

Some of the writers Maurin quoted blended romanticism with their social criticism. They were thoroughly anti-bourgeois and opposed the new age of industrial liberalism , rapid industrialization and the social convolutions it caused. They longed for the return of an age that as Carlyle said , "was concerned with mutual helpfulness not mutual hostility". According to Carlyle the new phrases which had entered the nineteenth century vocabulary, such as "fair trade", "free competition", and the "open market place" were nothing less than "due laws of war which society was waging upon itself". Some people who heard Maurin or read his essays, even some at the Catholic Worker house, tended to dismiss him as a dreamer or a misplaced romantic. His ramblings on Carlyle or Joseph de Maistre tended to support this view. But those who dismissed Maurin because he was a "dreamer" missed the point. Although some of the writers Maurin quoted were not exact in their perceptions, they did have an intuitive sense that something was extremely wrong with industrial capitalism. The legacy of political and social upheaval in the twentieth century has proven them right on that issue.

Secondly, Maurin only cited the so-called "Romantics" because he agreed with their criticisms, not necessarily with their solutions. Maurin was in and of the twentieth century. He did not long for the return of an idyllic past. His Catholicism did not betray a desire to return to the Middle Ages or to a theocracy. Rather his faith was an affirmation of a spiritual and social idea which transcended time. Therefore, when Maurin began to formulate his synthesis he relied far more on modern Catholic thinkers than on Thomas Acquinas, Duns Scotus or Augustine of Hippo. The group of thinkers on whom Maurin built his philosophy have yet to be completely absorbed by modern scholarship but that does not diminish the significance nor the originality of their work. Among the writers who gave substance to Maurin's thoughts were Peter Kropotkin, Leon

Bloy and Emmanuel Mounier. A brief glimpse at these three provides an idea of Maurin's own views of social and economic institutions and how they ought to be.

Peter Kropotkin, born in 1842 to Russian nobility, abandoned his birthright at an early age and joined the Russian underground. In nineteenth century Russia the cause of the revolution was the burden of the intellectuals. Kropotkin remained faithful to this cause all his life and when he died in 1921, his funeral became the last great demonstration against the new Bolshevick regime which had usurped and altered the revolutionary view of the majority of the Russian intelligensia. Kropotkin was recognized as one of the leading intellectuals of the left, yet he did not subscribe to the ideas of Marx or Darwin which dominated the thoughts of his collaborators. In his major work, *Fields, Factories and Workshops,* he proposed the idea that alienation and class division did not represent the natural state of humanity. He maintained that the great accomplishments of the past occurred in workshops where craftsmen and scholars worked in harmony. Kropotkin advocated a decentralization of the working place so that scholars and workers might once again join together in the enterprise of human creation . One of Peter Maurin's most used phrases, one which caught the imagination of unemployed students in the thirties was a direct quote from Kropotkin: "Scholars should become workers so that workers can become scholars".

In one of his "Easy Essays" Maurin paraphrased a key section of Kropotkin's work, and concluded that a major reason for class polarization is that the modern worker is:

> left without vision.
> And the worker left by the
> scholar without vision
> talks about liquidating
> both the bourgeois and the scholar.
> The scholars must tell the workers
> what is wrong

with things as they are. . .
The scholars must collaborate
with the workers. . .
The scholars must become workers
so the workers may be scholars.[6]

From Kropotkin, Maurin borrowed the Russian
narodnik idea of educating the worker, from Leon
Bloy, a fellow Frenchman, he found the roots of
his ideas on voluntary poverty. Bloy, an artist-
turned-writer, spent most of his time during the
decades around the turn of the century in Paris.
He lived in the artists' district of Montmarte
within the shadow cast by the grand church of the
Sacred Heart which was built on the spot where
Ignatius Loyola and his friends founded the
Society of Jesus. Among the many philosophers
and students who found their way to Bloy's small
house were Jacques and Raissa Maritain. The former recalled climbing the unending stairway to
the great Sacre Croix, bearing with him "that
distress which is the only real product of modern
culture." He found Bloy in a small house set in a
garden which reflected the tastes of another age.
Maritain dates his conversion to Christianity
from the time of this encounter when Bloy taught
him that there was only one true sadness in life
-- not to be born a saint. "All else became
twilight ." Maritain recalled.
In his writing, Bloy bludgeoned the
bourgeois scheme of life with images of the sublime virtue of voluntary poverty. He contrasted
the beauty of the lives of those saints who
rejected the lure of materialism with the "offal"
of the lives of those who live for the pursuit of
wealth. His writing had a profound effect on a
younger generation of writers living in France
around the turn of the century . Perhaps Maurin
who was selling newspapers on the streets of
Paris at this time also came into contact with
this spiritually powerful man. He certainly had

---

[6]Maurin, *The Green Revolution*, p.14.

read Bloy's works before coming to America, since his concept of voluntary poverty had a tremendous influence on his own development. And according to Arthur Sheehan, Maurin's first biographer, it was Maurin who introduced the work of Leon Bloy to this country.[7]

Bloy reveled in the power of the saints. "Saint Francis was not a poor man", he wrote, "He was in need of nothing since he possessed his God and lived through the ecstacy outside the world of senses." Bloy's idea of voluntary poverty was not new; it is at least as old as the monastic orders, but placed in the context of the early twentieth century, it was a sublime yet solidifying protest against bourgeois materialism. Maurin captured this theme in one of his essays when he noted that "while destitution isolated men, poverty as exemplified by the saints and monks of past ages bound them together."

Bloy's contribution to modern intellectual history is that he influenced and anticipated a later generation of Catholic writers who led a post-war Christian revival in Europe in the twenties. Among those influenced by Bloy was Emmanuel Mounier who in turn contributed to the ideas of Peter Maurin. In his book *The Personalist Manifesto*, Mounier wrote a chapter entitled, "Capitalism as Enemy of the Person". In it he states that the "economic organism underwent a sudden proliferation at the close of the eighteenth century and like a cancer it has eaten away the rest of the human organism." This "accident" as he called it, caused the majority of thinkers and men of action to proclaim the primacy of economics over history and regulate their actions according to this primacy. Such a juxtaposition, he maintained, "tainted the whole organism of the person and society so

---

[7]Arthur Sheehan, *Peter Maurin: Gay Believer*(Garden City, N.J.: Hanover House, 1959), p.70.

thoroughly," that all social disorder can be traced to it.[8]

Mounier believed that the modern age which witnessed the ascendance of economic man also saw the rise of corporate capitalism, the corporate state and socialism. Although these new expressions of order were designed to fulfill human needs more completely, they imposed an artificial community at the expense of individual dignity. In order to counter this drift in history, Mounier proposed a philosophy which emphasized the spiritual dimension of the person. This philosophy he called "Personalism". More than a platitudinous motto broad enough to cover the political passions of its varied participants, one historian has described it as "a term which conveyed the direction in which the majority of the membership thought speculative emphasis should be placed." Since ideology had been moving in the opposite direction, a defense of the human person seemed to be the proper direction for intellectuals of the Catholic left.[9] Personalism in France provided a Christian response to the rising tide of existentialism in Europe, and in the United States it entered a more practical dimension by providing the philosophic basis of the Catholic Worker movement.

By the beginning of the twentieth century as the work of Bloy, Mounier and others permeated various groups of Catholic thinkers, European Catholics began to clarify their philosophical opposition to the excesses of capitalism and socialism. A similar response from Catholics in the United States did not evolve. American

---

[8]Emmanuel Mounier, *The Personalist Manifesto*(New York: Longman, Green and Company, 1938), p.165.

[9]John Hellman, "The Opening to the Left in French Catholicism, The Role of the Personalists," *Journal of the History of Ideas*, 34 (July, 1973): p.387.

Catholics, for the most part, lacked the history and the intellectual tradition of Paris. But the European response to capitalism did finally arrive in America via the mind of Peter Maurin, and it was promulgated through a paper he co-founded, *The Catholic Worker*.

Many at the Catholic Worker minimized the role that Peter Maurin played in the development of Catholic Worker ideology, but to do so denies the historic significance of the movement. It was started by Dorothy Day a socialist-turned-Catholic, and Peter Maurin, a French Catholic immigrant. The socialist had little theology and the French immigrant could find no Americans who could accept his views. They were both looking for something that at the time did not exist: a Catholic movement with a Catholic view of economics, society and history. Failing to find it, they found each other, and from this meeting came the intellectual and spiritual form they both sought, or at least a close approximation of it.

To summarize, Maurin's philosophy was based on three ideas: history, the Church and the person. As the nineteenth century romantics, Maurin believed in the humanizing potential of history and tradition. Most of Maurin's contemporaries believed that tradition was useless. The new social science promised a more exact, useful and ordered view of humanity. But the new social science simply documented fragmentation by categorizing differences within social structures. The new social science could not measure that which denied quantification . Therefore the immeasurable human spirit, the stuff on which community is built, was factored out of modern history. Consequently, an age which witnessed unprecedented material growth suffered at the same time a great spiritual decline. In the nineteenth century the English writer Thomas Carlyle mourned the passing of the hero from history. And as the philosopher Ernst Cassier has pointed out Carlyle's "hero" was not simply the yearning for an idyllic past, but rather an existential protest against the demise of the "whole man" of body and soul. Maurin viewed the past similarly. But while Carlyle sought intangible heroes, Maurin found the clearest model of the entire person in the body of the Catholic Church. In a world reduced to raw statistics, the Church maintained the dignity and spiritual potentiality of the human race. In a world suffering from fragmentation the Church offered the vision of human solidarity. It was Maurin's hope to reintroduce the solidifying potential of the Church to the fragmented twentieth century. This was a formidable task, for Maurin had to go beyond the human blemishes of the Church which the new social scientists had put under a microscope. He had to search for the true spirit of the Church which for two thousand years had provided sustenance for those seeking community and human solidarity.

He rediscovered the Church which had built hospices for the poor and the pilgrim, and the Church of the monks who demonstrated the inherent unity between spiritual and economic life. When anarchists spoke of dynamite, he pointed out that the real dynamite was the social message of the Church. "If the Catholic Church is not the dominant social dynamic force", he said,

> it is because Catholic scholars
> have failed to blow the dynamite
> of the Church.
> Catholic scholars have taken the dynamite
> of the Church
> have wrapped it up in nice phraseology,
> placed it in a hermetic container
> and sat on the lid.[10]

Finally, Maurin deduced from the Catholic thinkers of Europe that the revolutionary potential of the Church would only be realized through the person. This idea was as old as Christianity. Its basic premise was that neither mass technology, mass politics nor mass movements

---

[10]Maurin, *The Green Revolution*, p.2.

would redeem history but that redemtion would only occur to the degree that individuals perfected themselves. The model of perfection to which these personalists adhered was Jesus Christ. Once again Christ was resurrected, this time by twentieth century scholars and activists who saw in his life the triumph of human solidarity.

Maurin worked out his philosophic synthesis while living in America, but the roots of his ideas extended deep into the soil of France. He was born into a large peasant family in the province of Bordeaux. The strong Catholic traditions of family and region must have had had an important influence on him, for when he was a teenager he joined the Christian Brothers, a religious order dedicated to teaching. He discovered his life's profession early, for as Dorothy Day often recalled, "Peter was always the teacher." But he could not continue to pursue his vocation in France for continual calls from the military became too disruptive, and in 1909 he joined 34,000 other Europeans who migrated to the New World that year.

This journey began what his biographer called a six year period of "extreme personal hardship." Initially he moved to Western Canada where he attempted to set up a homestead, but this ended in failure. He soon traveled to the United States where he drifted for the next few years taking odd jobs including one as a laborer for the Frick coal mining company and another as a janitor in a Chicago apartment building. His experience gave him a close view of the human cost of America's rapid industrial development. Unlike most of his fellow immigrants who accepted demeaning work for the promise of future prosperity, Maurin questioned a system which seemed to subjugate everything, even human dignity, to the pursuit of material gain. The disparity of values in America must have agitated the Weltanshauung of the French peasant. In 1914 he settled in Chicago and while supporting him-

self as a French tutor, he began developing the
ideas which would provide the intellectual foundation of the Catholic Worker movement. Record-
ing his early days in Chicago, Dorothy Day wrote,
"he read constantly, he walked, he taught. . .,
he wrote out his ideas in neat lettered script
duplicated it, distributed it himself on the
street corners and invited debate."

Maurin continued to develop and proslytize
his ideas, but in the prosperous war and post war
years he attracted few followers. The closest
his ideas ever came to becoming actualized
occurred in 1932 when he presented his program to
Dorothy Day, a young journalist and convert to
Catholicism. In the late twenties Maurin had
gone to New York to propagate his philosophy of
work. He frequented Union Square, a gathering
place for radicals of every political persuasion.
He would distribute his hand-printed pamphlets
and invite a debate with whomever happened along.
In addition to challenging political radicals,
Maurin would speak wherever he could get himself
invited. He even addressed Rotarian luncheons.
He also travelled to Columbia University to test
his ideas against the university's philosophers
and historians. Among the hosts to Maurin at
Columbia was the noted historian Carlton Hayes
whose views of history were somewhat similar to
Maurin's.

On one occasion, his travels took him to the
offices of *Commonweal* magazine editor, George
Schuster. He attempted to convince Schuster that
he ought to transform his magazine into a radical
Catholic journal. Unprepared for such a departure, Schuster suggested to Maurin that he discuss the idea with Dorothy Day. She had contributed a number of articles to *Commonweal* and
he was sure that she would be interested in his
proposal.

In November 1932, on returning home from the
Washington hunger marches, Dorothy Day found
Peter Maurin waiting for her. She remembered him
as a shabby looking man wearing a khaki shirt,
stained pants and a large overcoat with pockets

stuffed with pamphlets and loose papers. "When he started looking for something he pulled glasses out of his pocket [magnifying glasses which he ha purchased along the Bowery for thirty cents] and perched them halfway down his nose." At first she was perturbed by his intrusion, but as she listened to his ideas she became intrigued. Especially interesting to Dorothy was the prospect of publishing a periodical which focused on Catholic social thought.

Unlike other Catholics at the time, Dorothy Day was intellectually prepared for Maurin's theology. Born in Brooklyn in 1897, into a newspaper writer's family, Dorothy had travelled and lived with her family in San Francisco and Chicago before settling on her own in New York. In her early twenties (her age corresponded to the deacade) she began writing for the socialist paper The New York *Call*. Later she was a staff member of the *Liberator* and although she never officially joined the Socialist or Communist Party, she did share their view and dream of a harmonious world of workers who shared the fruits of their labor. Malcolm Cowley remembered her during the early twenties and recalled that "no one had more compassion for the downtrodden than she." Floyd Dell, in his autobiography, described her as that "charming enthusiast with beautiful slanting eyes." She along with her friends, took the inevitability of the revolution for granted, they "watched its progress", she recalled, "and were thrilled by its victories." She lived in a world "where dreams came true, where there was a possibility of the workers beginning to take over the means of production and starting to build that kind of society where each received according to his need and worked according to his ability."

She joined pickets and went to jail. She enjoyed her friends and the camaraderie of their shared vision. She remembered hanging around Provincetown Playhouse where Eugene O'Neill and other friends had rehearsals. Afterwards they would all meet in the back room of a saloon on

Fourth Street and Sixth Avenue, nicknamed "Hell Hole" by its customers. Here, she recalled, "Eugene O'Neill, Terry Karlin, an old Irishman who had known the Haymarket martyrs, . . .Mike Gold and others, were my constant companions". Often they sat on the ends of piers singing revolutionary songs in the starlight night, "dallying on the park benches never wanting to go home." In love with all mankind, they took back to their apartments men sleeping on park benches and gave them whatever bed was available.[11]

In addition to her social conscience, a strong spiritual sense had also always been fundamental to her personality and would eventually become her most dominant characteristic. She remembered as a small child "being afraid of God, of death of eternity, afraid of nothingness."[12] These feelings remained with her into adulthood and as a result she eventually abandoned her lover, her friends and what they called her rationality, and sought solace within the Catholic Church. Although she found spiritual tranquility within the Church, her social conscience remained troubled. The very winter she joined the Church she had been working with the Anti-Imperialist League, a Communist affiliate, but her recent conversion meant she had joined the side of the enemy. As she admitted her newly discovered refuge was clearly lined up with "property, the wealthy, with the state, with capitalism [and] with all forces of reaction."[13] Her inability to find an outlet for her social concerns within the Church had been particularly troubling to her on her journey to the Hunger Marches in Washington D.C. While witnessing the marches, feelings of alienation overwhelmed her. Once she revelled in the solidarity of such demonstrations. She was still anti-capitalist,

---

[11]Dorothy Day, *Long Lonliness*, p.85.

[12]Miller, *Harsh and Dreadful Love*, p. 37.

[13]Day, *Long Lonliness*, p.119.

but now her new faith forbade her from joining her Communist friends. What had troubled her more however was the apparent fact that the Catholic Church had turned its back on the needs of the poor. She felt compelled to agree with Bakunin who described Christianity as the "religion par excellence, because it exhibits and manifests to the fullest extent, the very nature and essence of the religous system, which is the impoverishment, enslavement, and annihilation of humanity for the benefit of divinity."[14]

Peter Maurin's view of the Church filled the void which Dorothy had felt since the time of her conversion. She was ready to plunge into the work he outlined, but Maurin hesitated. First, he felt she must have a Catholic education and background. After their first meeting he visited often, always with "books, papers, digests and articles which he either read aloud or left [with Dorothy] to read". During this time she had been working on some magazine articles so she visited the library daily. Upon arriving home however there was Peter, she recalled, "waiting to indoctrinate me. He stayed until ten when I insisted that he had to go home." He followed her around the house talking. If she were getting supper, washing dishes, or ironing clothes, it did not matter, he continued his lectures.[15]

Throughout the winter of 1933, Day planned her new Catholic journal, and finally on May 1, with funds she should have used for the rent and utlities, she published the first issue of *The Catholic Worker*. Along with some students she took the paper down to Union Square to distribute. Fifty thousand people were gathered there for the traditional Workers' Day celebrations. It was perfectly logical, but also heroic to distribute the new Catholic publication there. They were harassed and ridiculed to such an extent that all but one of her helpers departed, leaving

---

[14]*Ibid.*,p.172.

[15]Day, *House of Hospitality,* p.xvi.

her alone with Joe Bennet, "a tall gangling young man who occassionally had to sit down because of exhaustion that came from a heart damaged by rheumatic fever".

Peter Maurin did not like the first edition of the paper. He did not even like the name. He thought that after his months of instruction that Dorothy Day would publish a paper on Catholic philosophy. Instead, she had published a paper under a Catholic banner that exposed every social injustice under the 1930's sun. "Everyone's newspaper is no one's paper", he criticized. But Americans are less ideological than their European cousins. Dorothy was right. Unless the paper addressed practical issues it would not survive.

Dorothy and Peter could not have been more opposite. She was an urbane journalist, he an immigrant peasant. He was raised in a French Catholic tradition almost as old as the Faith itself, she was a recent convert. He was past midlife, she was a young single parent. Yet together they filled a great void in American Catholicism. Maurin was a Catholic philosopher in the European tradition, and Dorothy Day, the convert, was an articulate social critic. They represented two rare types in the American Catholic Church at that time, and together they contributed an important chapter to the intellectual history of the Catholic Church in America.

CHAPTER II

THE CHICAGO BEGINNING

The Catholic Worker movement developed in the fecund environment created by the intellectual ferment of the 1930's. The generation which came of age during this decade could hardly feel sanguine about the future their parents and grandparents had bequeathed. Faith in material progress which had been nurtured by the technical miracles of the nineteenth century, hardly seemed relevant to a generation whose own immediate experiences included a world war and a great economic depression.

Seen in this light, the Catholic Worker movement of the 1930's represented one more alternative for a world shaken from ideological complacency. This anxiety was not limited to those living in the United States, nor did it originate there. Throughout Europe new ideas of order were attracting mass movements, particularly among young people, who with strong convictions, arm bands and bugles joined together to rebuild a world that their parents had left in shambles. They marched for a new order that would eliminate war, class struggle and poverty. A powerful but tranquil state provided the centerpiece for this new vision of community which would end the disorder caused by the bourgeois individualism of the nineteenth century. Since old meant corrupt, tradition was scrapped. There were new politics, new history and new sociology, all of which provided blueprints for a new vision of the future. Despite varied means and semantics, young fascists, communists and socialists all shared the same desire for this common end.

American upheavals in the thirties mirrored those in Europe. American complacency, already shaken by the war, collapsed in the years of the Great Depression. And in the thirties, a Europe

which most Americans had viewed as fatally dis-
eased only a decade before, became a fountain of
truth for many who believed that America too, was
old enough for a renaissance.   From New York's
Union Square to Chicago's Bughouse Square, and in
every town park in between, ideologues hawked
their intellectual wares to whomever would
listen.

At the forefront of these would-be social
architects were thousands of unemployed college
students who had taken advantage of cheap tuition
at state universities to escape the blue-collar
world of their parents, only to discover upon
graduation that the Depression had swallowed up
the high paying jobs they sought. This surplus of
unemployed students caused the Catholic Worker,
as well as other movements to swell rapidly in
the mid 1930's.   Peter Maurin's declaration that
"scholars should become workers so that workers
could become scholars", appealed to many idle
students. One professor who was an unemployed
college graduate at the time recalled that
Maurin's principle "struck the imagination of a
great number of unemployed graduates who came to
hear him."   The Catholic Worker principles of
"voluntary poverty . . , and living among the
common people gave new purpose to many disillusioned college students who hoped to influence
the masses."[1] Dorothy Day believed that it was
solely because of these young people that the
Catholic Worker prospered in the 1930's.   Because
of these students, Dorothy Day recalled, "before
we were many years old we had thirty two houses
around the country."[2]

The Chicago Catholic Worker developed from
this aggregate of frustrated but enthusiastic
students.   From its very beginning the Catholic
Worker had an avid albeit fragmented following in

---

[1]C.T. Echele, *Peter Maurin: Christian Radical*(St. Louis: Pio Decimo Press, 1950), p.7.

[2]Studs Terkel, *Hard Times* (New York: Avon
Press, 1970), p.349.

Chicago. People there had encountered the Catholic Worker in various ways. John Cogley first learned about it when he discovered a crumpled copy of the *Catholic Worker* in a church pew. He recalled "being startled by the down to earth writing and simple woodcuts. . . scattered through the eight pages". Ade Bethune's artwork particularly impressed Cogley. "It had life and strength", he later wrote, "especially her representations of the saints whom she depicted while sweeping floors or mending pots, not simply standing around in spiritual idleness."[3]

Father John Hayes, at the time a teacher at Quigley Preparatory School, distributed copies of the *Catholic Worker* to his students to provide material for class discussions. Hayes, who became an important figure in the movement, admired "Dorothy Day's forthrightness in attacking problems of the depression as few Catholic leaders had previously done". He was also impressed with her "simple devotion to Christian principles and her willingness to live according to them."[4]

In spite of the enthusiasm for the movement in Chicago, prior to 1936 it remained fragmented. Until that year followers of the Catholic Worker participated in the movement by reading the paper and sending donations to the Catholic Worker House in New York. After June, 1936, however Catholic Worker enthusiasts in Chicago had their own house and soon their own paper. The original impetus came from a visit by Peter Maurin to Chicago in the early summer. Shortly after Maurin's visit, an article appeared in the New York *Catholic Worker* calling for the formation of a Catholic Worker group in Chicago. This invitation came from Arthur Falls, who had introduced a new column in the paper that month entitled

---

[3]John Cogley, *A Canterbury Tale*(New York: Seabury Press, 1976), p.4.

[4]Interview, Msgr. John Hayes, Chicago, Illinois, June 14, 1976.

"Chicago Letter" . Taking advantage of the enthusiasm generated by Maurin's visits to various churches and schools, Falls reported that there had been a "healthy awakening" of the Catholic social concience in Chicago. He reported in the New York *Catholic Worker* a number of student protests against the exclusion "of Negroes from Catholic Schools", and he related these incidents to increased circulation of the *Catholic Worker* and to the appearances of Dorothy Day and Peter Maurin in the Chicago area. In this same article he called for the formation of a Catholic Worker group in the Chicago area "not only to further interest in race relations, but in all other social and economic problems with which our Catholic people show an appalling lack of knowledge." [5]

Arthur Falls was a product of the great heritage of black Catholics in New Orleans. Upon moving to Chicago, he involved himself in the Civil Rights struggle and by the 1930's he had become the chairman of the Human Relations Commission of the Urban League. As an organizer, he was eager to enlist any group which might strengthen the cause. For this reason, the Catholic Worker received his attention. He himself was a Catholic, but until the *Catholic Worker* appeared he had never seen a paper with a Catholic banner advocating racial harmony and condemning lynching and segregation in such uncompromising terms. "In fact," he admitted in an interview years later, "until the appearance of the Catholic Worker, my colleagues and I often considered the Catholic Church to be on the side of the enemy on race issues."[6]

When he first discovered the *Worker*, Falls wrote to its editor and confessed that he was "struck with wonder by the paper's content. Certainly those who have labored with Catholics

---

[5]*Catholic Worker*, June, 1936.

[6]Interview, Arthur Falls, Western Springs, Illinois. June 9, 1976.

24

both of the clergy and laity in an effort to get them to face practical issues, are more than joyful to see your publication." He had one suggestion for the paper. He thought it would be interesting to "see one of the workmen at the top of your page to be a colored workman."[7] Dorothy Day accepted his suggestion and the masthead remained unchanged throughout her lifetime.

When Falls wrote to Dorothy Day and told her he had been "laboring" among Catholics, he meant just that. This was a time when priests would refuse to administer the sacraments to blacks, advising them to go to their "own colored priests", and most of Chicago's Catholic schools remained segregated.[8] With the appearance of the Catholic Worker movement and paper, Falls finally had members of his own faith on his side of the civil rights issue. For too many years, he felt, he had stood alone as a Catholic advocate of racial justice. With this in mind, Falls took the lead in starting the Catholic Worker movement in Chicago. He hoped to attract young people to the movement, indoctrinate them, and turn them loose on their parish priests and teachers who often were propagating their own prejudices on the issue of race.

Falls did not have a difficult time finding interested and enthusiastic followers. Although economically stagnant, the Depression years were intellectually fertile. Ed Marciniak who would be drawn to the Catholic Worker, remembered these years as a time when "young people were really alive." He and his friends "would read avidly, especially every learned Catholic magazine [they] could locate." The journals became the basis for discussion sessions that sometimes went on "from Sunday afternoon to early Monday morning: one week Maritain, the next the steel strike." Early

---

[7]*Catholic Worker*, June 1933.

[8]William Osborne, *The Segregated Covenant* (New York: Herder and Herder, 1967) p.105.

the next morning they returned to their homes, "exhausted, but tremendously stimulated."[9]

Not an exception, Marciniak's memories characterize an era when people attempted to grasp meaning in a world which in their lifetimes had shifted gears from the speed of horsecarts to that of airplanes. Cognizance of the acceleration of time had become popular knowledge in the thirties, and if people could not slow it down they at least wanted to determine direction.

Marciniak and his friends also reflect another trend of the 1930's. They were part of the first generation of Catholics to attend college on a large scale. Catholic colleges swelled in that decade as thousands of young people representing the collective struggle of their immigrant parents for upward mobility sought quality higher education at both the high school and college levels. The Catholic Worker was not the only product of the intellectual energy of the thirties. Other groups such as the Chicago Interstudent Catholic Action (CISCA), the Catholic Youth Organization (CYO) and the Catholic Family Life group which organized after the Second World War, all developed as a result of an educated Catholic laity working with an enlightened clergy. Within a few decades, the Catholic generation that came of age during the Depression and Second World War transformed the Church from a refuge for immigrants into a powerful body of articulate spokesmen prepared to struggle for human rights at every level, from the street corner to the White House. The "Catholic Revolution" as it was referred to in the 1960s and 1970s, has its roots in this generation. And when historians search for causes of the radical transformation of the Church over the last half century, the immigrant hod carriers, maids and stock yard laborers who worked overtime to secure the dream of education for their children can not be ignored.

---

[9]Dan Herr, "Chicago Dynamo," *Sign* (September, 1962): p.12.

Onto fecund groups such as Marciniak's the invitation to start a Catholic Worker house in Chicago fell. Marciniak remembered that when he discovered the Catholic Worker, "a whole new world opened up." For the first time he saw "Catholics around the country giving themselves to help the poor. . . right the wrongs of injustice."[10] For these reasons Marciniak as well as many others joined Falls in the basement of St. Patrick Church in late June 1936 to organize the Chicago Catholic Worker movement. The personalities at the first meeting varied greatly, and not all shared the vision of the Marciniak's in the group. Many attended because they were familiar with Dorothy Day and her work in New York City. But others came simply because they noticed the word "Catholic" or "Worker". Consequently, the group included one woman who after a quick inspection of the assembly, left hastily exclaiming in a loud voice, "Just because I'm a Catholic it doesn't mean I have to associate with Niggers!"[11] Another person at the meeting used the occasion to explain to the working class Catholics the sins that the Church had perpetrated against them, and that their only refuge was the Communist party.[12]

Interest or curiosity was not the only reason attracting people to the first Catholic Worker meeting. Many came simply because food and refreshments had been promised. Despite claims to the contrary which appeared regularly in the *Chicago Tribune*, economic problems continued to wrack Chicago as well as the rest of the nation. Even though George Young, president of the Chamber of Commerce, promised in 1935 that the city could expect to "make great strides in the near future"[13], the American Federation of

---

[10]Ibid.

[11]Falls interview.

[12]Ibid.

[13]*Chicago Tribune,* January 5, 1935.

Labor claimed in the Spring of 1936 that across the nation over eleven million people remained unemployed.[14]

Even if a person were able to secure a job, the newspapers would not allow him to forget the grim economic realities of the decade. Gangsters still dominated Chicago's headlines as some individuals chose extra-legal means to escape the consequences of the Depression. Lesser criminals also appeared in the paper as they too tried to lessen the burden of the economic collapse. In what became a familiar story in the thirties , the *Tribune* reported the arrest of a group of men who had broken into an emergency relief center. Tears ran down the face of one of the defendants, "I am a minister", Percy Dumas explained, "but I love meat, and I don't get enough of it on relief. I was tempted by veal chops and fell", he confessed.[15]

There were probably a number of people like Dumas at the first Catholic Worker meeting. They have always been an integral part of the movement, since their poverty remains the most obvious injustice which the Catholic Worker protested. Would-be social prophets from all over the city also came to the meeting. Although the first assembly was a confusing spectacle, a commitment emerged to keep the group alive. Thereafter, every Sunday a number of individuals led by Arthur Falls maintained weekly Catholic Worker meetings. In contrast to the first large assembly the ensuing meetings never attracted more than fifty individuals.

Falls gave a running account of the group's progress in the *Catholic Worker* each month, and in the October, 1936 issue he announced "the Catholic Worker in Chicago is looking for a house which will draw the man in the street as well as a place which can serve as a library and discussion center." A month later the Sunday before

---

[14]*Chicago Tribune*, June 9, 1936.

[15]Ibid., January 18, 1936.

Thanksgiving, the Chicago Catholic Worker opened a house in an abandoned storefront at 1841 Taylor Street. "We truly started from the ground up" Falls reported in the November *Worker*, "for we began with two chairs and a stove". Later Father John Hayes brought them some chairs for their meetings which Falls noted, "allowed us to rise up off the floor".

Although motivated by similar commitments, each Catholic Worker house varies greatly. These differences occur because each house reflects the personality of the individual or group responsible for it. The original Catholic Worker House in New York fed the hungry and sheltered the homeless which revealed Dorothy Day's compassion for the poor, a trait which accented her entire life. The house in Chicago however, was not Dorothy's. Falls had created it and in the early days his ideas prevailed. John Cogley, remembering those early days, described Falls as being more mature than the rest of the group. "He was more than a decade older" than most of us, Cogley later wrote, "which added a great deal of stature among a group of twenty-year olds". Although a black man , he made the group aware that "he could not be placed into the stereotype subservient Negro role to which most whites were accustomed at the time." He was, Cogley observed, "remarkably sophisticated, [and] almost patronizing to his inferiors".[16] Falls came from an old family in New Orleans which had produced a number of pioneering nuns and priests. Falls himself was a physician, and he had moved to Chicago where he spearheaded the early civil rights movement there. Although as concerned for the downtrodden as Dorothy Day, he disagreed with her methods. He was never enthused with the idea of feeding and sheltering the poor. Rather, he adopted the black bourgeois techniques of the time. To him the most appropriate goal was to give the poor the tools necessary to provide for themselves. Reflecting this idea of self help,

---

[16]Cogley, *A Canterbury Tale*, p.8

the first Catholic Worker house in New York replaced the customary soupline with an information center which contained pamphlets and books and suggestions for utilizing meager resources to their fullest extent. They also formed a consumer's cooperative and a nickle a week credit union.

Reporting in the *Catholic Worker,* Falls boasted that the new Catholic Worker house had a fine library which contained books on co-ops, race relations and similar topics useful to the neighborhood. He also explained that their credit union was making low-interest loans available to the poor. This union lasted until 1948 when it could no longer endure the burden of a treasurer who granted loans to people who deserved charity, but not necessarily credit.[17] The house that Falls started was not a house of hospitality within Peter Maurin's definition, and Dorothy Day must have grimaced more than once in that first year when she heard of Fall's projects being carried out in the name of the Catholic Worker, but at least the movement had finally taken root in Chicago.

At first the Taylor Street house was a loosely organized affair run by volunteers from the local high schools and cooleges. Eventually these meetings gained some significance in the community, as leading scholars sympathetic to the Catholic Worker movement spoke there when they were in Chicago. The forums became popularized by word of mouth and pamphlets, and soon visitors to the house included professors from the University of Chicago, Northwestern and Loyola as well as people from Bughouse Square, Chicago's version of New York's Union Square.

In addition to Jacques Maritain, who was leading a Thomistic revival at the University of Chicago at the time, other guest lecturers

---

[17]Falls reimbursed everyone who had invested in the union and then closed the books in 1948.Pamphlets, Accounts, Falls Private Papers; Falls interview.

included the Catholic sociologist, Paul Hanley
Furfey and the Benedictine liturgist, Virgil
Michel. Both these men had an important impact on
the Catholic Worker and on Catholic thought in
the 1930's. Furfey was one of the leading critics
of a group of sociologists who were labled
"scientific naturalists". Their hypothesis that
man could create a mechanized yet humanistic
society was being proven wrong, Furfey claimed,
in the social laboratory of Europe. As an alternative, Furfey proposed a personalist sociology.
He asserted that the human community could not be
improved by external manipulation but only by
individual personal commitment. It was the
enlightened person's duty not to compel positive
behaviour by force but rather by example. In the
introduction to his book he stated that the best
example of personalism in action in the United
States was the Catholic Worker movement.[18]
    Virgil Michel also spoke frequently at the
Catholic Worker house. Michel, an early advocate
of liturgical reform, felt that if the average
Catholic had a closer contact with the external
symbols of his religion, he would "see his
intimate connection with all creatures of the
earth and his responsibility to them." [19]
Michel's ideas occupied a fundamental place in
Catholic Worker thought, and Michel himself saw
in their movement "the promise for a more gentle
world."
    Through their round table discussions with
Catholic intellectuals and the practical application of a rudimentary personalism, the Catholic
Workers in Chicago and elsewhere were joining, at
least spiritually, the Catholic intellectuals of
Europe such as Nicholas Berdyaev, Emmanuel
Mounier and the Maritains, who were attempting to
formulate a Christian response to the rising tide

---

[18]. Paul Hanly Furfey, *Fire On Earth* (New
York: Macmillan and Co.).

[19]Virgil Michel, "Personality and Liturgy,"
Oratre Fratres, 13 (February 19, 1938): p.156.

of atheistic existentialism. Today with a "personalist Pope" and the institutionalization of
liturgical reform their actions seem somewhat
commonplace, but in the 1930's the Catholic
Workers were wandering into hitherto unexplored
intellectual and cultural regions. And it was in
Catholic Worker houses such as the one in Chicago
that many Catholics first heard the words "personalism" and "liturgical reform". In Chicago in
the 1950's when the liturgical movement gained a
great deal of momentum, the people who were leading that movement were the same ones who had
started the Catholic Worker more than a decade
earlier.

The scope of the Sunday forums at the
Catholic Worker house went beyond the realm of
what most would classify as "Catholic thought".
For example, John Cogley recalled that a young
automobile worker from Detroit who had recently
spent some time on the assembly line in Russia
addressed their group. His name was Walter
Reuther, the same man who would be president of
the United Auto Workers in the post World War II
era. These seminars, which attracted activists
and scholars of varying degrees, often resulted
in animated arguments. For many of the young
Catholics present it was a strange yet exciting
experience. For the first time they were experiencing the radical dimension of their Faith.
Previously they perceived their religion as a
source of comfort not confrontation.

These Sunday meetings also attracted their
share of eccentrics, a trademark of every
Catholic Worker house. One who frequented the
meetings on Taylor Street was Joe Diggles, who,
much to the chagrin of good Catholics present,
declared that he was a devout Catholic and a card
carrying Communist. Eventually Diggles was
expelled from the Party, not for his errors
regarding Catholicism, but for supporting those
"traitors" to the working class, the union people
that went on strike during the Second World
War.[20] Another "character" who visited the

---

[20]Sullivan interview; Hayes interview.

Catholic Worker and eventually dominated the
house on Taylor Street until his death in 1950
was John Bowers. He entered a Catholic Worker
meeting one Sunday attired in fancy clothes and
adorned with a walking cane, kid gloves and a
diamond stud tie pin. After listening to a
speaker extol the virtues of the "people" for
over an hour, Bowers finally rose, and in his
piercing voice exclaimed, "Given the chance, the
masses will make asses of themselves!"
     Bowers who frequently could be found debat-
ing radicals at Bughouse Square, did not look or
act the part of a social activist. With his well
manicured mustache, Italian cigarillo clenched
between his teeth, and his overcoat draped over
his shoulders, he looked more like a con man than
anything else. He soon became a regular around
the house and would thrill younger members with
stories from his limitless imagination. He told
them he knew Mae West personally, also the Bar-
rymores, but he was not speaking to Lionel due to
a recent argument they had had. Just before
Dorothy Day made her first visit to the Taylor
Street house, Bowers revealed that he had known
Miss Day from her Greenwich Village days, and
that he also was a close friend of Ernest Heming-
way, Gene O'Neill, and Scott Fitzgerald. But the
faith of even his most avid believers was shaken
when Dorothy Day arrived and in no way resembled
Bowers' description.
     The quick tongue which announced his arrival
at the Catholic Worker house soon became his
trademark. When Dorothy Day once suggested that
it seemed a little incongruous that he sport
fancy clothes and fine jewelry while working
with the poor, Bowers responded in the words of
Diamond Jim Brady, "them that has 'em wears 'em!"
Another time when he heard someone praising the
work of the Baroness de Hueck, he informed everyone that she was no baroness at all, but "a
Polack from Brooklyn!" His lack of respect for
the woman who had done such courageous work in
the area of racial justice, probably left the
group stunned.

In addition to his biting remarks, the question of Bowers' source of income added another dimension to his mystique. When he first began to visit the house he had a gentleman's job walking around Marshall Field's department store catering to the whims of the rich clientele. But the salary from this job could harldy cover the expenses of his expensive Hyde Park apartment or his fancy attire. Those closest to him could only guess from hints that he lived off a moderate family inheritance. Soon he gave up his worldly comforts, moved into the Catholic Worker house and took over the administration of it. Until Bowers' arrival, the house was only a part-time enterprise, since no one had the time to live there and give it a sense of permanency. Bowers' presence changed that and after he moved in the house became more available to the community.

It is difficult to ascertain what motivated a man like Bowers to undertake such a project. Father John Hayes, an early supporter of the Catholic Worker in Chicago, surmised that Bowers at middle age, had found his life lacking substance and the Catholic Worker filled the void he felt. His closest friend at the Worker, Tom Sullivan, described him as a scholarly type who had made "tremendous strides in the life of the spirit". Whatever his motivation, there was more to Bowers than an initial confrontation with his quick tongue revealed. He remained at the Catholic Worker house, and eventually shed his fancy attire for the more ragged clothing characteristic of those who knocked on his door every day. Taylor Street was his final home and Bowers soon became one of the minor heroes of the Catholic Worker movement.

Bowers' harsh exterior and his barrage of sarcasm from which everyone suffered, made it difficult to understand what attracted him to the Worker movement. One hint that his harsh exterior overshadowed a more benevolent character was the affection he had for the children in the Taylor Street neighborhood. Soon after moving

into the house he began a day care center, where
he organized projects for neighborhood children.
Also, under Bowers' direction, Catholic high
school and college girls held classes on Saturday
at the Taylor Street house. In addition to tutoring school work, the young women held sewing,
cooking and drawing classes for the children.
Bowers also collected and contributed funds of
his own to help pay the tuition for black children to attend the previously all white St.
Ignatius school. Bowers had instigated his own
integration program and the tutoring sessions on
Saturday were planned to assure its success. One
of the reasons blacks were excluded from the
schools was the assertion that they were
intellectually inferior to the white children.
Bowers took great pains to make sure that excuse
would no longer prevail.

Another of Bowers' projects was the Maritain
supper club. This "club" allowed Bowers to
indulge himslef in two of his favorite pastimes:
cooking and lecturing. These meetings took place
every Monday night. Bowers cooked an exotic meal
with food he purchased from one of the ethnic
grocers in the neighborhood. He charged only
twenty-five cents for the meal , but the guests
had to remain silent during the dinner while
Bowers read from the works of Maritain. After
the meal there were the obligatory discussion
sessions on Maritain, which were not discussion
sessions at all but rather monologues delivered
by Bowers, which was just as well, for as Jim
O'Gara recalled , "No one really had the
slightest idea of what Bowers was talking about!"

Word of the Maritain supper club reached the
University of Chicago and a group of professors
attended one evening at the invitation of a student. Everyone was glad to have the professors
there since they would probably fill the embar-
rasing void that always followed Bowers' call for
questions. In the middle of the lecture, one of
the professors raised a question regarding a
point Bowers had made. In response, Bowers
feigned a cough, announced that he had a

35

LIBRARY ST. MARY'S COLLEGE

headache, and ended his lecture. The professors caught the none-too-subtle hint and left the meeting. After their departure, Bowers continued with his lecture, commenting that those who had just left had probably only come for the cheap meal.

Bowers eventually dominated the Taylor Street house, but during its first year of existence it was still primarily Arthur Falls' project. The most obvious sign of Falls influence was the ever recurring organizational meeting. Everyone belonged to a committee. There was one on education, which reported Bowers work with the neighborhood children, as well as efforts by members to introduce discussions on integration into their classrooms. There were also committees on liturgy, labor and cooperatives. Falls hoped that each committee would "carry out an active program in their particular field, spreading not only the sale of the paper but also the philosophy of the Catholic Worker." Soon, he felt, the Catholic Worker would "attain a place among the leading civic groups in the city."[21] This stress on organization and growth and acceptance within the community, was more a reflection of Falls' personality than Catholic Worker philosophy, which had always been decentralized if not downright anarchistic. The emphasis on organization left John Cogley as well as others, cold. He had been attracted to the movement because of its philosophy of voluntary poverty and personal charity. But as it was turning out, he later wrote, "we were running a kind of conference center with religious overtones." Aside from Bowers' work with the children, the Taylor Street house was nothing but a

---

[21]For a good contemporary account of the goals and direction of the early house on Taylor Street see Joseph Morrison, "Chicago Catholic Worker Movement," (Masters Thesis, Loyola University of Chicago, 1938).

LIBRARY ST. MARY'S COLLEGE

place "which sponsored forums or committee meetings five nights a week."[22]

Cogley was not the only one becoming disillusioned. The personalism of the Catholic Worker seemed to many to be lost in the entrapments of bureaucratic procedure. Young people were attracted to the Worker because they believed it was in the intellectual vanguard. But the Chicago Catholic Worker, with its committees, forums and growth plans, had taken on many of the bourgeois characteristics they abhored. Cogley and other malcontents received support for their criticisms when Dorothy Day visited Chicago. Perhaps she came precisely because she shared their discontent. Cogley noticed that she was "obviously not pleased with the way things were going on Taylor Street". There was "really nothing wrong with the program", he later wrote, "but a bit of conventional social work among children and numerous committees did not coincicide", he was sure, with "Dorothy Day's idea of how the Catholic Worker should be running in the nation's second largest city."[23] Even Arthur Falls agreed that "Dorothy never really agreed with my concept of the Catholic Worker" but he maintained, "I thought it was the more realistic approach."[24]

Dorothy Day was forty years old when she visited the Chicago Catholic Worker house for the first time, and as Cogley remembered her she was "a strikingly attractive woman." Even though she had not "achieved the spiritual authority that marked her later years", Cogley noted, "she was well on her way." He could not help but notice her effectiveness in "prodding young people to achieve greater heights of spiritual development" which "she combined with detachment and social concern." One of the most memorable nights in

---

[22]John Cogley, *A Canterbury Tale*, p.10.

[23]Ibid.

[24]Falls interview.

Cogley's young life occurred when he, Tom Sullivan and Dorothy Day dined together at a cheap
restaurant. "She told stories of her friendship
with Rayna Prohme, Emma Goldman, Eugene O'Neill,
John Reed, Carolyn Gordon and practically every
other social activist of the previous generation." He never forgot how "glamorous the whole
evening seemed. . .and of course to us", he
recalled, "she was too."[25]

   Dorothy must have been impressed with
Cogley also, for before getting on the bus back
to New York, she gave him the keys to a house she
had rented on Wabash Avenue. She had paid the
rent for the summer in hopes that he would be
able to start a Catholic Worker house of
hospitality there. The house was located in the
middle of a black ghetto and she hoped that
Cogley and others might be able to augment the
work being done there by the priests at St.
Elizabeth parish. Cogley recalled that day as
being the greatest of his young life. "At last we
were behaving as we were supposed to, we were
finally in the true Catholic Worker movement. It
was great to be so young and feel alive and be
participating in something so vital."[26]

   His enthusiasm did not last long. The first
night at the house a knock on the door at three
in the morning starled him from sleep. He looked
out the window and saw a weary disheveled woman.
His "first homeless guest", he thought, and
opened the door to welcome her. As it turned
out, the woman had travelled a great distance and
was looking for the people who used to live in
the house Cogley was in. Since it was late, the
woman accepted Cogley's invitation to spend the
night, but in the morning she left in search of
her relocated friends.

   This incident became the first of many disappointments for Cogley at the house on Wabash
Avenue. He soon realized that the pastor of St.

---

[25]Cogley, *A Canterbury Tale*, P.12.

[26]Ibid.

Avenue. He soon realized that the pastor of St. Elizabeth Church did not need his assistance. Unlike many fortress-like recotries of the day with forbidding entrances, this one's door was always open, and Father Drescher always kept lunchmeat and bread on the table for anyone that wanted it. Families in the area knew the recotry well and were aware that they could always go there if they were in need of help. Father Drescher was also one of the few priests in Chicago at the time who played an active role in the civil rights movement. Cogley soon realized that the Catholic Worker house was a "fifth wheel" so when the rent expired at the end of the summer so did his house of hospitality.[27]

In spite of the failure, a break had been made from the Taylor Street house, and the collapse of the Wabash Avenue Project was but a preface to a more successful enterprise the following Spring. This split did not signal the end of the Taylor Street house; it merely meant that there would be two Catholic Worker houses in Chicago. The Taylor Street house continued to prosper with Bowers' influence becoming increasingly prevalent. Falls began to lose interest in the Catholic Worker house and under Bowers' direction it became more like a child day care center that a Catholic Worker house. Despite this departure the house remained significant in the history of the Chicago Catholic Worker, for it was through the house on Taylor Street that many Chicagoans first discovered the Catholic Worker movement.

---

[27]Ibid, p.12, 13.

CHAPTER III

CHARITY

After closing the Catholic Worker house on Wabash Avenue in August, 1937, John Cogley left for Ross, California where he joined the Dominican friars. But he remained there only a short time. On a cool morning in early December, Tom Sullivan stood in Dearborn Station and met the train that brought his friend Cogley back from California. Having left the seminary himself, Sullivan did not press the issue with Cogley, but rather just offered him a place to stay for a while. Tom Sullivan recalled this event in Cogley's obituary which he wrote for the *Catholic Worker* in June 1976.

The obituary revealed Sullivan's deep affection for Cogley, but there was more to this attraction than that which eminates from the heart. There was a bond of common ideas, dreams and disappointments. And it joined not only Cogley and Sullivan but Marciniak, O'Gara and a few of the others that pioneered the Catholic Worker movement in Chicago in the late thirties. Although different in many ways, each shared the spiritual instinct that their religion could be an instrument of social change. For this reason they all spent some time in the seminary. They felt that in the priesthood they could best implement their vision of religion as a social force. Had they lived in a time when ideas within the Church hierarchy coincided more closely to their own, these men might have pursued their vocations in a more traditional manner. But outside of a few exceptions such as Bishop Sheil, the founder of the Catholic Youth Organization (CYO) and Monsignor Reynold Hillenbrand, the director of the Archdiocesan seminary, the Catholic hierarchy and those responsible for training young priests remained a rather conservative group, the product of the American Catholic Church's immigrant history.[1] In many ways the socially active priests that first nurtured young Catholic activists in Chicago were an anomaly in the American Catholic Church.

Soon after returning to Chicago, Cogley took to the road again. He set his sights on the Catholic Worker house in New York City where he hoped to settle in, help out as much as he could and possibly write for the paper. Like the Muslim to Mecca, the Jew to the Wailing Wall or the Communist to Lenin's tomb, Cogley and other young Catholics like him in the thirties flocked to Mott Street in New York City. There at the Catholic Worker House they found a sense of comraderie only experienced by those with a common cause. At the Worker house young people spent their days helping with the soupline or selling the *Catholic Worker*. New York's streets blossomed with idealists throughout the depression. Walking near Union Square one could often hear hawkers screaming "Read the *Daily Worker!*" and frequently a nearby salesman would retort "Read the *Catholic Worker* daily!"[2]

In the evenings the young Catholic Workers sat around their storefront home discussing economics, politics, philosophy and religion. These issues remained at the core of their spiritual and intellectual life. The day's activities

---

[1]As Jay Dolan has pointed out in his survey of American Catholicism, the period from 1890 to 1950 was marked by conservatism which eminated from the immigrant nature of the Church. During this period priests and hierarchy alike tended to emphasize the ritual and order of the Church over its social message. Because of this Catholic liberals such as Cogley chose alternate outlets for the exercise of their religious conscience. Jay Dolan, The American Catholic Experience (Garden City: Image Books, 1987), pp.384-388.

[2]Dorothy Day, *Loaves and Fishes* (New York: Curtiss Press, 1960), p.24.

sapped their abundant energy, and the evenings restored it. Years later Dorothy Day recalled, "those early days, that early zeal, that early romance, that early companionableness, how strongly they all felt it."[3]

By 1938 the depression had once again over-whelmed those on the fringes, and the Catholic Worker again began to feel the strains of abject poverty. The house became so crowded that Cogley and a few of the young men spent the entire night walking the streets of New York in order to leave more beds available for the homeless. They wandered as far as Central Park, keeping them-selves awake by singing, telling stories and walking. At daybreak they met Dorothy Day on the way to mass. Attendance at Mass was fundamental to these young people. "The Catholicism of the Catholic Worker went unquestioned" John Cogley later recalled, "the young people may have struck their fellow Church members as too insistent on drawing out the full social implications of the Faith, but they were observant and devout"[4] Upon returning from Church the young men assisted at the breadline. When the work was completed, they would collapse, exhausted, into one of the beds just vacated by its Bowery occupant.

Cogley enjoyed his stay in New York. It allowed him to be part of a movment he felt to be in the intellectual vanguard of the 1930's. But soon it became apparent to him that he should take his energy and commitment elsewhere. There was a surplus of people at the New York Worker house, and when Cogley received an invitation to help with a new house back in Chicago, Dorothy Day suggested that he go. Cogley was somewhat disappointed; he had hoped to remain in New York and write for the paper. In his memoirs, he

---

[3]William D. Miller, *A Harsh and Dreadful Love: Dorothy Day and the Catholic Worker Move-ment*(New York: Liveright, 1972), p. 95.

[4]John Cogley *A Canterbury Tale* (New York: Seabury Press, 1976), p.22.

wrote, "My own inclination was to stay where I was, but everyone agreed that I was needed in Chicago, and no one suggested that I was indispensable at Mott Street. Until the last minute I secretly hoped someone would suggest that I might write for the paper, but no one did. My journalistic calling had not yet been recognized by anyone but Peter Maurin". In June 1938 he boarded a bus and returned to Chicago.[5]

His destination was 868 Blue Island Avenue where Al Reser and Ed Marciniak had started a new Catholic Worker house at about the same time Cogley had left for New York. This new house differed greatly from the one on Taylor Street. Following the model of New York, it had abandoned committee meetings and forums for a breadline and shelter. The building they occupied does not exist anymore. The area has become part of the University of Illinois Circle Campus. But in 1938, urban renewal remained far in the future, and the area was populated by poverty stricken families of various nationalities.

The building which housed the Catholic Worker had been an old factory. The walls were brick and the floor was made of rough unfinished wood. On the first floor, small offices were located in two corners and on one side there were five steps which led up to the main floor. In this larger area they built a kitchen, and for a time allowed the men to sleep on the floor there. Above the room there was another floor which served as the main sleeping area . Al Reser lived in the house and eventually his friend Marty Paul joined him. Marciniak also used his influence as president of CISCA to enlist young Catholics into the project.

An acronym for Chicago Inter Student Catholic Action, CISCA was a federation of Catholic student groups in the Chicago area. Directed by Father Martin Carrabine and Sister Cecilia Himbaugh, this organization became a center for Catholic student social action. In the

---

[5]Cogley, *A Canterbury Tale*, p.22.

1930s, under Cardinal Mundelein and his Auxiliary Bishop, Bernard J. Sheil, small groups in Chicago became a model for the nation in Catholic social action. Whereas many bishops would have attempted to silence priests and religious such as Carrabine, Himbaugh and Hillenbrand, the hierarchy of Chicago cultivated these hybrids. The result was a generation of activists thoroughly committed to both social reform and to their faith. From the C.Y.O. "hotels" for homeless youth to the complex system of social organizations directed by Msgr. Reynold Hillenbrand at St. Mary of the Lake Seminary, Chicago provided a fecund environment for the development of a Catholic social conscience among the laity. This ambience provided not only the enthusiastic energy needed to start the Catholic Worker in the 1930's, but also many of the well known liberal Catholic leaders of the next generation.[6] In the October 1936 issue of the *Catholic Worker*, Arthur Falls mentioned the presence of Carrabine's group at the Catholic Worker meetings and noted that they were "going to make Chicago Catholic Worker conscious to an amazing degree".

Without the enthusiasm of youth the house on Blue Island Avenue may never have gotten off the ground, because it began with much hope, and little else. But Marciniak knew that "Dorothy Day had started a house on a shoestring in New York" and he was certain "that the thing could also be done in Chicago"[7] The building rented for thirty dollars a month but Reser convinced the landlord to give it to them for fifteen, he also secured two months rent free in exchange for

---

[6]Edward Kantowicz, *Corporation Sole: Cardinal Mundelein and Chicago Catholicism*(South Bend: Notre Dame University Press, 1983), pp.189-216.

[7]*Chicago Sunday Times*, January 29, 1939.

cleaning the building.[8]

In the early spring of 1938 they occupied
the building which they Christened "St. Joseph
House of Hospitality". Their adopted patron came
to their aid immediately. When they began to
look for food, they met a devout old Italian man
who ran a local food store. " I give you credit"
Joe Iscabucci told them in broken english, "St.
Joseph see you pay me!" Although the payments
often came late , the grocer continued his
deliveries and his devotion to the Saint. On one
occasion when a considerable amount of time
passed between payments , Cogley noticed the
little man gazing at the statue of St. Joseph .
Somewhat concerned, Cogley asked Joe if something
was wrong.

"I am asking St. Joseph to send you some
money so I can get paid!" Iscabucci replied.

On Good Friday in 1938 the new Catholic
Worker house opened its doors and a "seemingly
endless line of humanity shivering from the early
morning frost, shuffled in for the initial break-
fast of boiled oats, hot coffee and corn bread."
In addition to the hundreds they fed that first
morning, they also took in their first guests.
Within a short time they were feeding over three
hundred fifty men a day and housing most of them.
The older men slept on cots donated by a group of
nuns, and the floor provided beds for the
younger men, who were grateful to be sheltered
from the penetrating wind which blew in from Lake
Michigan.

"It was a bitter winter" Cogley recalled,
and the place was chock full [of] men wedged in
like cigarettes in a pack, it was heartbreaking
to tell another hundred standing outside the
door, shivering and pleading, that there was no
more room and they would have to 'carry the banner' for the night."[9] Before the Catholic Worker

---

[8]Cogley, *A Canterbury Tale*, pp.14-15; John
Cogley, "Store Front Catholicism," *America* 79
(August 21, 1948): p.447.

[9]Cogley, "Storefront Catholicism," p.447.

was a few months old the group became absorbed
into the relief crisis of the Summer of 1938.
The resurgence ofthe Depression in 1937, and the
refusal of the state legislature to recognize the
reappearance of the problems of economic recession, left the relief centers of Chicago completely depleted by the late Spring of 1938. And
the fact that summer was late arriving that year
aggravated the problem. Convening in crisis, on
June 2, the legislature held what the *Chicago
Tribune* called "its most intensive field day on
the problem of relief in years." But the legislature, unprepared to solve the problems of
recession, excused themselves from them. They
used the emergency meeting to produce "figures
purporting to show that [the legislature] could
not divert any more of the treasury surplus for
relief."[10] Mayor Edward Kelley and the anti-
machine governor, Henry Horner spent the entire
month of June arguing the question of relief and
responsibility. One compromise which emerged,
much to the chagrin of the city merchants, was a
revenue-producing license on all public business
establishments. But this plan could not with-
stand the onslaught of lawyers representing the
many chambers of commerce throughout the state.
On June 14, the bill failed and businessmen
rested easily while thousands of unemployed
remained locked out of relief centers. As the
crisis worsened, the Catholic Worker house on
Blue Island Avenue became locked into a depression within a depression. Relief stations continued to close or cut allowances, and those at
the St. Joseph house, along with other private
charities throughout the city, girded their belts
and anticipated the worst.
     During this crisis public funds became so
scarce that the Director of the Chicago Housing
Authority reported that "large dogs in the animal
shelter were receiving more per meal than men on
relief."[11] With thousands abandoned on the

---

[10]Chicago *Tribune*, June 3, 1938.

[11]Terkel, *Hard Times*, p.444.

streets, the Catholic Worker house squeezed in
over three hundred and fifty men every night into
their two-story abandoned factory. In addition,
they secured credit at a local hotel which lodged
fifty more. In the morning after serving break-
fast they scrambled around the city begging for
money to pay the hotel so that their credit would
be good for one more night.[12] During the day they
also organized groups of unemployed workers for
demonstrations. Borrowing a chapter from the Communists, they organized the workers into the
"Catholic Union of the Unemployed". Marty Paul
organized the group and they picketed the local
relief office with signs demanding that the
director reopen it.[13]

By July, when the problems of the unemployed
still had not gone away, the recalcitrant legislature and reluctant governor allowed the mayor
of Chicago to divert a portion of the revenue
from gasoline taxes in the city to supplement the
depleted relief fund. The governor also discovered a surplus in the treasury which allowed him
to deposit an additional 2.8 million dollars into
the relief centers of Chicago.[14]

The change of heart came suddenly and
without explanation. Apparently the administration in Springfield decided that there was no
political capital to be gained in the exploitation of human suffering. Chicago's City Hall
may have been full of corruption, but the
unfortunates on the street had little to do with
it. In an interview with Studs Terkel, one
relief director had another explanation; he figured that the merchants had finally agreed to
support a relief project because they thought

---

[12]*Chicago Catholic Worker*, June 1938.

[13]Marty Paul interview; *Chicago Catholic Worker*, June 1938.

[14]*Chicago Tribune*, July 2, 1938.

shoplifting costs would go down if the homeless had a place to go and a meal to eat.[15]

Despite the government's action, the poor areas of the city had experienced over a month of suffering and the young Catholic Workers had witnessed firsthand the grim realities usually disguised in statistics. The scenes of tragedy they saw would remain a lifetime. Years later, John Cogley remembered one man who had spent several nights sleeping in a damp alley way because the city was unable to renew his shelter ticket. They brought the shivering man into the Catholic Worker house and filled him with warm soup. When this did not stop him from trembling, they rushed him to nearby Cook County hospital, but they were too late and the man soon died of bronchial pneumonia. Many others flocked to the house to avoid the certainty of death from exposure. One man died there and the stench of another threatened to drive everyone out of the house. The odor came from the man's foot which was rotting from frostbite. Even after years had passed, Cogley could recall the "stench of unwashed bodies, and the filthy clothes. . . , the eerie nightmares. . . , and . . . the shouts of troubled sleep." [16]

By the middle of July the newly allocated funds began to trickle into the public relief centers and the tardy summer weather finally arrived also. As the burden of crisis lifted from the Catholic Worker house, they began to plan new projects. First they decided to publish a paper to express their ideas, report activities and most importantly, to provide income. This idea took root mainly because of the arrival of John Cogley, who brought with him from New York his unfulfilled desire to be a journalist.

The paper they published had a format identical to the *Catholic Worker* in New York. The only difference was the word Chicago in the mast-

---

[15]Terkel, *Hard Times*, p.444.

[16]Cogley, "Storefront Catholicism," p.447.

head. As with the orginal, the Chicago paper
sold for a penny a copy. Despite the
similarities, they were quick to emphasize they
were not competing with the New York paper. The
first editorial stated , "If you have one quarter
[the cost of a yearly subscription] remember, to
Mott Street with it, where Dorothy [Day], Peter
[Maurin], and Bill [Callahan] are doing the best
job of Catholic journalism in the country." But,
it continued, "if you have two quarters, take a
chance on Blue Island Avenue, we shall do our
best." They also reprinted a telegram from
Dorothy Day which encouraged them with a "Go
ahead and God Bless you!"[17]
     In addition to reporting activities around
the house and issuing appeals for funds, the
Chicago Catholic Worker, edited by Marciniak and
Cogley, contained articles on personalism, church
liturgy, unions, labor conditions in Chicago,
movie and book reviews and reports on experiments
in communal farming. The editors wrapped their
articles in Catholic theology, yet it was done
with a taste and style that brought them compli-
ments from many distinguished Chicago writers
including Carl Sandburg.
     An informal survey in the May 1939 issue
reported that their paper had a circulation of
ten thousand which included college students,
college-educated adults, and priests. During
labor strikes they always published extra editions and handed them out on the picket line.
     After reading the paper, Dorothy Day wrote
that the Chicagoans' work far "outshines our own
poor effort".[18] Although this self effacing
remark was typical of Dorothy Day, the new
journal was quality work, and although it could
be argued that much of what appeared on social
issues was already being printed elsewhere, it
was not appearing in the Catholic context in
which this paper placed it. By the Fall of 1938,

---

[17]*Chicago Catholic Worker* June 1938.

[18]*Catholic Worker*, May 1939.

the young people who started this house were well
on their way to careers which would mark their
entire lives. They were pursuing the struggle of
social justice under the mantle of Catholic
theology. In Europe they would have been one of
many, but in America they remained distinct if
not unique.

CHAPTER IV

RACIAL JUSTICE

In 1933, an ambulance rushed a car accident victim to the closest hospital, which happened to be Catholic. The woman was refused admission because of her color. She was rushed immediately to Cook County Hospital where she died the next day. Shortly thereafter, an angry doctor wrote that the woman probably would have lived had she received immediate treatment.[1] In the post World War II era, Catholic clergy and laity played a leading role in integrating the city of Chicago, but prior to the war, the Catholic Church in Chicago, for the most part, remained a segregated institution.

In the first decades of this century, when blacks began moving to northern cities in great numbers, the Catholic Church remained officially indifferent, and the laity greeted them with outright hostility. Although wrong, Catholic antipathy for blacks had deep seeded roots. Even prior to the Civil War, Catholics feared a mass movement of freed slaves north would threaten their jobs. They also were hostile to the abolitionist movements of the nineteenth century because of their alliance with anti-Catholic groups.[2] Confronted with the mass migration of blacks at the turn of the century, the Bishop

---

[1]Arthur Falls, "Honesty in Race Relations," *Interracial Review* (September, 1933): p.159.

[2]Richard Lamanna and Jay J. Coakley, "The Catholic Church and the Negro," in Phillip Gleason, ed., *Contemporary Catholicism in the United States*, (South Bend: University of Notre Dame Press, 1969), p.148; William Osborne, *The Segregated Covenant* (New York: Herder and Herder, 1967), p.201; Oscar Handlin, *Boston's Immigrants* (New York: Atheneum, 1974), p.201.

gave them a parish of their own at Thirty Sixth and Dearborn Streets. He brought in a black priest from Peoria and left this part of his congregation to fend for themselves.[3]

Between 1915 and 1920, increased migration of black Catholics from Louisianna swelled their number in Chicago significantly. This rapid growth caused a great deal of anti-black sentiment among white Catholics, and in response to this, Archbishop George Mundelein "formulated a policy that resulted in almost complete racial segregation within the Archdiocese of Chicago."[4] Ignoring the traditional geographic boundaries which normally determined parishes, he made St. Elizabeth Church at Forty first and South Michigan Avenue an all black parish. Wary of his own priests' reaction to assignments there, he invited a missionary priest into the diocese to tend to the needs of the black members of his flock.[5]

The parish was located within blocks of what was then described as the heart of the black belt, Forty seventh and South Park Avenue. Here it was said in the thirties if you were looking for "a certain Negro in Chicago, stand on the corner of 47th and Park long enough and your're bound to see him". One contemporary wrote, "There is a continuous movement here, shoppers streaming in and out of stores, irate tenants filing complaints, [and] job seekers moving in and out of the United States emplyment office." In addition, there were "tea pads, reefer dens, buffet flats and call houses known only to the underworld and those respectable persons, white

---

[3]Osborne, *Segregated Covenant*, p.204

[4]Alan Spear, *Black Chicago* (Chicago: University of Chicago Press, 1967), p.179; Osborne, *Segregated Covenant*, p.204.

[5]St. Clair Drake and Horace Clayton, *Black Metropolis*(New York: Harcourt, Brace and World, 1970), p.379.

and colored, without whose faithful support they could not exist."[6]

In this neighborhood St. Elizabeth parish grew, prospered and became the largest black parish in the United States. It became the religious center for all black Catholics regardless of where they lived. If a black Catholic wanted to have his child baptized, his daughter married, or his parents buried, St. Elizabeth parish is where he went. By the mid-thirties, the population of black Catholics had expanded to the point where they comprised sizable minorities within at least twenty parishes in the archdiocese. No longer able to restrict attendance to St. Elizabeth church, Cardinal Mundelein allowed pastors of the churches involved to establish their own racial policies. Most of these priests, reflecting the prejudices of their parishoners, maintained policies of segregation. Black Catholics were permitted to attend mass, but parish sodalities, clubs and schools remained closed to them.[7]

This predjudice displayed by the Catholic Church caused many black leaders in the thirties to consider it to be one of the major obstacles in their quest for racial justice. Even Catholic schools denied the implications of the truths they taught. Aside from Loyola and De Paul Universities, all Catholic Schools in Chicago were segregated in the thirties.

Arthur Falls led the Catholic Worker movement into the struggle for racial justice. He found racism among his coreligionists to be not only deplorable but contradictory to the principles of Catholicism. The Catholic Church, he wrote "had set out in unmistakable terms the foundations of justice and charity . . . and the

---

[6]Ibid., pp. 380-381.

[7]John La Farge, *The Race Question and the Negro* (New York: Longman Green and Company, 1943), pp. 156-157; Osborne, *Segregated Covenant,* p.205.

duties of Christians toward their fellow man."
No true Catholic could fail to be interested in
race relations, he advised, "because the very
word 'catholic' means universal and all-
embracing".[8]

Falls had been chairman of the Interracial
Commission of the Chicago Urban League since
1932. Organized in 1919 after the great race
riot that year, the Urban League had been considered by the white community as a "citadel of
safe leadership". This opinion changed in the
thirties, however, as a younger more vociferous
group of black activists, such as Falls, began to
take over the leadership of the movement and to
support "non-violent patterns of aggressive
action".[9] Being a Catholic, Falls wanted to
enlist the powerful influence of the Church into
the civil rights cause, but up to the thirties it
had remained an indifferent witness to prejudice.
To counteract this drift, he helped organize the
Catholic Interracial Foundation in the Spring of
1934. Dorothy Day was vice president of this
organization until the early forties when it
became an all black movement. Arthur Falls was
associate editor of the Foundation's publication.
The paper was an attempt to awaken Catholics to
injustices suffered by blacks and raise their
sense of obligation to these members of the human
community.[10] From the beginning, the Catholic
Interracial Foundation remained close to the
mainstream of the civil rights movement, but it
never made inroads into the white Catholic community as Falls had hoped. The main accomplishment of the *Interracial Review* was that it served

---

[8]Arthur Falls, "Catholic Obligation to Fight
Racism," *Interracial Review* (October, 1933):
p.184.

[9]Drake and Clayton, *Black Metropolis*, p.734.

[10]Lamanna and Coakley, "The Catholic Church
and the Negro," p.156.

notice to other members of the black press that
not all Catholics were racists.[11]
It was not until Falls discovered and
eventually established the Catholic Worker in
Chicago that he had a strong Catholic ally in the
civil rights struggle. According to Falls, "The
Catholic Worker proved to be the key with which
Negro Catholics were able to open the door of
white churches in Chicago".[12] Years later, John
Cogley wrote about the Catholic Worker and its
contributions to the civil rights movement in the
thirties. "Although the Catholic Worker did not
coin the phrase "Black is Beautiful", it [the
Catholic Worker movement] acted as if it knew it
was. In hostels that grew up under its auspices
blacks and whites lived together easily and
mingled freely without self-conciousness or any
note of do-goodism."[13]
Cogley's first Catholic Worker house had
been in the heart of the black community, and now
in the new house on Blue Island Avenue, he, Marciniak and others joined with Falls in his struggle for racial justice. The first target was the
Catholic schools. They invited teachers to round
table discussions on integration strategy.
Despitd the offical attitude of pastors and
school advisory boards, the majority of Catholic
school teachers advocated integration. These

[11]Ibid., pp.156-157; Harold Ley,
"Catholicism and the Negro," *Christian Century*,
(December 20, 1944) pp. 1476-79.

[12]Falls interview; the role played by the
Catholic Worker in confronting racism in the
Church is documented in La Farge, *The Race Ques-
tion*, p.244; Lamanna and Coakley, "The Catholic
Church and the Negro," p157; Osborne,*Segregated
Covenant*, p.131; and David Obrien *American
Catholics and Social Reform: The New Deal Years*
(New York: Oxford Press, 1968), pp.202-203.

[13]*National Catholic Reporter*, October 30,
1968.

meetings at the Worker house served as both a means of moral support and as instruction for teachers who lacked the means and designs for taking on Church authority. It was through meetings such as these that many Catholics were first introduced to the concept of a strong laity and Catholic social action.[14]

As part of their plan, teachers sent their students down to the Catholic Worker Houses on Blue Island Avenue and Taylor Street. Arthur Falls recalled that "We indoctrinated these students". Armed with papal pronouncements and Church teachings, students would return to their classrooms with questions such as "In light of what the Pope has said regarding the right of every Catholic to have a Catholic education, why has this school excluded Negroes?" According to Falls, many teachers who avoided such topics for fear of reprisal were only too happy to discuss them when brought up by the students. In fact, aware that the students had been indoctrinated, teachers were well prepared with answers designed to enlighten students on questions of race and prejudice. Very few Catholic schools in the city were left untouched by this street theater propaganda and because of this activism, a new generation of Catholics in Chicago were developing different attitudes toward race relations. For example, Father Daniel Cantwell, a priest who helped lead the civil rights movement in Chicago in the 1940s and fifties, recalled that he first became involved in civil rights as a seminarian helping at the Chicago Catholic Worker in the late thirties.[15]

Falls also took some students with him to meetings of the Urban League and other activist groups with which he was associated. Through

---

[14]Martin Work and Daniel Kane, "The Layman and His Organizations,"in Gleason, ed., *Contemporary Catholicism*, pp. 356-359.

[15]Interview, Monsignor Daniel Cantwell, Chicago, Illinois, May 26, 1976.

Falls' initiation, many young Catholics for the
first time joined Chicago's urban reform movements. Until this time, Catholics were expected
to restrict their activities to Catholic groups,
and in the thirties Falls remembers a priest describing him as a "bad Catholic" because he sent
Catholic students to such meetings and families
to public relief centers instead of to their
local parish priest when confronted with conviction.[16]

His association with the Catholic Worker
also gave Falls the opportunity to publish his
views in a journal which attracted a
predominantly white audience. Although he had
been writing in the New York *Catholic Worker*
since 1936, he rarely discussed the race issue.
His column, "Chicago Letter", dealt primarily
with the progress of the Catholic Worker movement
in Chicago. On one occasion however, Dorothy Day
turned over the entire front page of the paper to
an article written by Falls entitled "Danger of
Race Riots in Chicago's Slums". Describing the
sordid conditions of black housing in Chicago,
Falls accused the Chicago Housing Authority of
working "in collusion with neighborhood improvement associations to exclude Negroes". In local
jargon, "neighborhood improvement associations"
were groups of whites who united to keep their
neighborhoods segregated. Long before the controversy arose in the fifties, he pointed out
in this article that the University of Chicago
was "buying property from people who might rent
or sell to Negroes in order to hold the line"
against black integration. He also pointed out
that the University of Chicago "actively supported the segregation policies of the Neighborhood Associations." In the mid-fifties when the
Hyde Park-Norwood Community Conference, supported
by the University of Chicago, proposed a plan for
urban renewal, it was hailed by a majority of the
liberal community of Chicago. The only formidable opposition came from a committee of

---

[16]Falls interview.

Catholics headed by John Egan. The only journalist who actively supported Egan was Ed Marciniak
who edited *Work*. Marciniak who was still a young
man at the time already had over a decade of
experience in civil rights activism which was
rooted in his early involvement with the Catholic
Worker movement. [17]

Hopeful of the impact that a paper with a
Catholic banner would have on the politically
conscious city council, Falls sent them copies of
the *Catholic Worker* issue on Chicago slums along
with a letter containing a "strong plea to make
possible equality of opportunity for Negroes in
housing".[18]»

When Marciniak and Cogley began their
Catholic Worker paper, Falls saw it as another
source of propaganda. He hoped to use his
influence over the young members of the group to
control the editorial policy so that the paper
would prioritize racial issues. Although he was
never able to realize this goal, Marciniak and
Cogley did give him space to elicit his views.
When, for example, the Anti-Lynching Bill became
filibustered in Congress, Falls urged readers to
"throw their solid support -- vocal, written and
actual-- behind the Gavagan-Fish Anti-Lynching
bill." He reminded readers that "13,000,000

---

[17] Marciniak and Egan opposed the program
because it lowered the amount of housing in the
area that belonged to blacks and it did not provide plans to relocate those who would lose their
housing. Of course these former Catholic Workers
were opposing what a later group of activists
would refer to sarcastically as "urban removal"
in the name of "urban renewal". For a favorable
report on the Hyde Park Project see: Robert Dentler, *The Politics of Urban Renewal* (Glencoe: Free
Press of Glencoe, 1961) For Marciniak's and
Egan's position see: Rossi and Dentler, *Urban
Renewal*, pp.225-239; also Marciniak papers for
texts of speeches opposing the proposal.

[18]*Catholic Worker*, May, 1937.

exploited discriminated, despised, black brethren of Christ are still calling out for fearless uncompromising Christians to set the pace and light the way". [19] In another issue he continued his attack on Chicago's discriminatory housing policies. Warning readers not to compare their racial attitudes favorably against the South, he told them that cities like Chicago have their own form of lynching, in the form of tuberculosis and rickets which result "from holding Negroes within rigid ghettos".[20]

Although the Archdiocese of Chicago would not organize an official interracial council until 1946, The Chicago Catholic Worker planted the seeds in January 1938 when they established monthly hearings on interracial justice at the auditorium of St. Elizabeth Church. These meetings, as Ed Marciniak recalled them were in the form of mock trials, and they received a great deal of attention in the neighborhood and the black press. For example, the *Chicago Defender* in a large page two headline announced "Chicago Catholics to hold interracial meeting." The paper described this event as "one of the outstanding meetings being held under Catholic Worker auspices". Eager to encourage white allies, the paper was lavish in their praise of the Chicago Catholic Worker, stating that their work was "helping to make Chicago a leading city in the promotion of racial harmony."[21] Arthur Falls probably drew more attention to the Catholic Worker than it deserved, but in these pioneers days of the civil rights struggle any activism at all on the part of Catholics in favor of blacks was a banner which Falls, a black Catholic was eager to unfurl.

As most early civil rights groups, the Catholic Workers designed their meetings for

---

[19]*Chicago Catholic Worker*, January 1940.

[20]Ibid.,March, 1941.

[21]*Chicago Defender*, January 8, 1938.

education rather than confrontation. But in the fifties and early sixties when priests and nuns waded with blacks into segregated beaches in Chicago, and picketed segregated Catholic clubs and hospitals, they traced the roots of their activism to the change of attitude they experienced as a result of their contact with the early Catholic Worker movement.

Ed Marciniak, who in the 1960's headed the Mayor's Committee on Human Relations, began his struggle for racial equality with the Catholic Worker movement. He organized the interracial hearings at St. Elizabeth auditorium, and a few years later was instrumental in founding the Interracial Council in Chicago. During these years the Chicago Catholic Worker as well as other civil rights groups utilized appeals to conscience rather than force, but this helped prepare them for the more active era that followed. Marciniak's work, particularly, in the early civil rights movement, won him support from people such as the black poet Claude McKay who wrote to him, "I like you Ed, because you are a natural, if you erred it would be on the side of right never on the wrong side". And in concluding he said, "I am certain that if you like a Negro you like him as a person and not because you feel you ought to mortify yourself to like one." [22]

In one of his "Easy Essays" Peter Maurin had written:

> Theologians say
> that Christ died
> for the redemption
> of the Negroes
> as well as
> the Nordics. The Nordics
> were created
> by the same Creator
> and redeemed
> by the same Redeemer
> as the Negroes.

---

[22]McKay to Marciniak, March 5, 1945, Marciniak private papers.

> The redeemed Nordic
> will enjoy
> the beatific vision
> in the same Heaven
> as the Negroes.
> The redeemed Nordics
> receive the same Christ
> at the altar rail
> as the Negroes.
> The redeemed Nordics
> belong to the same
> Mystical Body
> as the Negroes.[23].

What the Chicago Catholic Workers accomplished certainly pales when placed in the context of the civil rights struggles of the 1950's and sixties and it disappears completely when placed within the great panorama of black history. However, they added a significant texture to the relations between white Catholics and blacks by announcing the simple proposition that blacks belonged to the body of Christ and deserved the dignity of that distinction. Such a statement might seem commonplace, but in an era when the United States Senate could not even pass a bill making it against the law to lynch a man, it was a beginning. And their propaganda helped turn a generation of Catholics away from the prejudices of their parents, toward a new era of racial justice.

---

[23]Maurin, *Easy Essays*, p.97.

CHAPTER V

ANTI-SEMITISM

The most significant contribution of the Worker movement to Catholic history is that it involved their religion in human rights issues, an area where it had been conspicuously absent. This concern took on a special importance in the 1930's when Father Charles Coughlin's social justice crusade took on an anti-semetic flavor. According to Catholic historian David O'Brien, despite the temerity of many Catholic leaders, "the Catholic Worker always opposed Father Coughlin and took the lead [among Catholics] in fighting anti-semitism"[1] Ironically, Father Coughlin began his radio career defending his faith against demagogues in the twenties who wanted to drive Catholics out of the country. He went on the radio then to answer attacks that a local Klan group in Detroit had made against his religion. In those days his calm, mild voice appealed to reason. But in the decade that followed, as his radio audience expanded, so did his ambition, and he graduated from sermons to political speeches and finally to demagoguery. Although millions listened to the mellifluous voice of Coughlin in the thirties, his actual following remained small. Unfortunately, as John Cogley later pointed out, these Coughlinites became for many the archtypal urban Catholic immortalized in novels, plays, and short stories.[2] Their significance also became magnified in non-fiction, as some historians in the mid-fifties began to view the Coughlin phenomenon as the missing link between Populism, which they

---

[1]O'Brien, *Catholic Social Reform,* p.173.

[2]John Cogley, *Catholic America* (New York: Dial Press, 1973), p.78.

described as home-grown fascism and McCarthyism.[3] Whether the Coughlinites deserve such distinction is doubtful, but certainly these extremists, although a minority, were vocal enough, and their actions violent enough, to make American Jews wonder if the tragedy their relatives were suffering in Europe would be repeated in their own country.

In the late thirties, as Coughlin's remarks became more inflammatory, many early listeners turned away in disillusionment, but his audience was replenished by zealots.[4] Most noticeable of his new followers was a group of young toughs who called themselves the "Christian Front". Coralling their hate under the banner of Christianity, they waged a crusade of vengeance against Jews and Communists alike. They organized anti-Jewish boycotts, and carried signs and distributed leaflets which urged people to "Think Christian", "Act Christian" and "Buy Christian". They also organized "gun clubs" and practiced military techniques in preparatiuon for the day when they would be required to defend Christianity and Americanism with their lives.[5]

Although the main strength of the movement remained in New York, its reverberations were

---

[3]Peter Vierick, "The Revolt Against the Elite", in Daniel Bell, *The Radical Right*(Garden City, N.J.: Doubleday and Company, 1963), pp. 135-154; Victor Ferkiss, "Populist Influences on American Fascism," *Western Political Quarterly*, 10 (June, 1957):pp.350-373.

[4]Cogley, *Catholic America*, p.96; Marciniak interview. According to Marciniak, Coughlin unintentionally swelled the ranks of the Catholic Worker during those days when many who had been attracted to the priest because of his early stands on social justice, became disenchanted with his anti-semitism.

[5]*Voice*, August 1940. This paper was published in the early forties as a Catholic response to anti-Semitism. See pp.79-80.

felt thrpoughout the country, reminding Jews of previous persecutions at the hands of Christians.[6] The anti-Defamation League of the B'nai B'rith, American Jewish Congress and the Jewish Labor Committee waged a vigorous campaign of counter-propaganda against the Christian Front. An example of their work was a book published under the auspices of the "American Jewish Committee" called *Father Coughlin, His Facts and His Arguments*. In a section of this book entitled "Catholic Response to Anti-Semitism, the book relied heavily on material taken directly from the *Catholic Worker*, for during these years of trial, the strongest Gentile opposition to the "Radio Priest" and his followers came from the Catholic Worker movement.

In July, 1939, *Social Justice*, Coughlin's newspaper, carried a headline announcing Christian Front plans to launch a full-scale membership drive in the city of Chicago. But as the *Chicago Catholic Worker* pointed out in January 1940, "the movement never got much of a foothold" in their city. One reason for the Front's failure was the condemnation of the group by Cardinal Mundelein. Although striken by an illness which would soon take his life, the archbishop garnered enough strength to launch an attack both written and verbal against Coughlin and his political activities. The priest was not "authorized to speak for the Church", Mundelein warned, nor did his "views represent the doctrine or sentiment of the Church". Too ill to continue his assault on Coughlin, Mundelein had his state-

---

[6]Charles Tull, *Father Coughlin and the New Deal* (Syracuse: Syracuse University Press, 1965), pp.207, 244; Cogley,*Catholic America*, pp. 96-97; O'Brien, *Catholic Social Reform*, p. 157.

ment condemning Coughlin read on national radio by Bishop Bernard Sheil..[7]
Another reason for the failure of the Christian Front in Chicago was its inability to attrct young men in their late teens and early twenties into the movement. In New York they had provided strength and the greatest numbers to the Christian Front, but in Chicago these young people had other diversions. The national C.Y.O (Catholic Youth Organization) was just beginning to blossom under Bishop Sheil's tutelage, and CISCA also attracted a large number of young Catholics..[8] For those of a more extreme or romantic nature there was the Catholic Worker. "Students have been a wonderful help", Cogley wrote in his column. "They come down on Saturdays and help clean house, and feed men who but for circumstances may have been a brother or a father"[9] Those inclined to extremism also found a home at the Catholic Worker. One high school student took pleasure in thrilling members with stories of his confrontations while selling copies of the *Chicago Catholic Worker*. Once he and some friends were arrested in Aurora for

---

[7]Tull, *Father Coughlin,* p.203. George Flynn, *American Catholics and the Roosevelt Presidency*(Lexington: University of Kentucky Press, 1968), pp.185-186. Flynn emphasizes Mundelein's close association with Roosevelt as a reason for Mundelein's criticism of Coughlin, but Mundelein, whom John Cogley described as "one of the most outstanding bishops in American Catholicism", felt more was at stake in the Coughlin controversey than political expediency; Cogley, *Catholic America*, p.153.

[8]Roger L. Treat, *Bishop Sheil and the C.Y.O.* (New York: Julian Messner Inc., 1951), pp vii-xi; Father Carrabine, a director of CISCA was also a member of the Committeee of Catholics to Fight Anti Semitism.

[9]*Chicago Catholic Worker,*March, 1940.

selling the papers. "Of course they [his
friends] were a little nervous this being their
first time in jail" he reported. "The police
wanted to know about this 'Peter Maurin
agitator'" , who appeared as the headline story,
but after "we propagandized them", he bragged,
"they let us go."[10]

The Catholic Worker, both in Chicago and New
York, also waged a journalistic war against
Coughlin and the Christian Front. "It has become
quite the thing these days to be anti-Semetic"
John Cogley editorialized. "Suddenly, people who
never gave it a thought are discovering that the
Jew is to blame for all their troubles".[11] In
another editorial addressed to "Our Jewish
Readers", Cogley apologiged for the "rotten
situation" of having to admit the anti-semitism
of some Catholics. "Our duty", he wrote, "is to
fight it with charity and justice." Catholics
seemed to have forgotten, he concluded, that in
the words of Pope Pius XII, "Spiritually we are
all semites."[12]

Coughlin did not ignore the criticism of the
Catholic Worker. As early as 1937, his paper
Social Justice, warned that a "fake headline of
the *Catholic Worker* misleads [the] American working man". Although the paper bore a Catholic
name and quoted papal encyclicals, he said that
the paper's position on the Spanish Civil war
alone (the *Catholic Worker* was neutral) was
enough to "make one wonder if the thing were not
downright Communism camouflaged in Catholic
paint." Coughlin even joined with Patrick Scan-
lan, editor of the *Brooklyn Tablet*, in an attempt
to persuade the Archbishop of New York to suppress the *Catholic Worker* [13]

---

[10]Ibid.

[11]Ibid., December 1938.

[12]Ibid., June 1939.

[13]*Social Justice*, July 5, 1937; Miller,
Harsh and Dreadful Love, pp.142-153.

In an open letter to Coughlin in the *Chicago Catholic Worker*, Cogley attacked the priest for the anti-semitism he perpetrated through innuendo, misquotes, and slander. Cogley received national attention as a writer for the first time when Coughlin reprinted this letter in his own paper, *Social Justice*. In its edited form, the letter appeared polite enough and was used by Coughlin to emphasize his contention that his attacks were directed against "bad" Jews only and "good" Jews ought to be left alone. It was a theme which appeared frequently in his broadcasts. For example on Sunday, December 4, 1938, he told listeners that anti-semitism was not the issue, "decent Jews. . . must repudiate atheistic and international Jews." Although Jews in America could hardly take comfort from such distinctions, Coughlin's equivocal remarks did influence many Catholics into thinking that a certain degree of anti-semitism was patriotic. One listener even wrote to Dorothy Day to chastize her for her criticism of Coughlin. "Shouldn't we know the truth about the Jewish situation?" she asked. And defending Coughlin she wrote, he "was most careful to make a distinction between the good Jew and the bad Jew".[14]

In the edited form of Cogley's letter which received national attention he wrote, there were "people who don't have much sense who have rallied beneath your banner." These people, he continued have used "your controversial Russian figures to justify a senseless, unChristian attitude toward Mrs. Cohen, the delicatessen lady around the corner , and Mr. Meyer, the insurance collector. . ." the priest should set these wrong minded people straight, Cogley advised, and "help make up for the pain and insult many innocent Jews have received from your confused followers."[15]

---

[14]M.S. to Dorothy Day, n.d. "Catholic Worker Papers", Marquette Archives Milwaukee, Wisconsin.

[15]*Social Justice*, May 22, 1939.

The edited version of the letter tempered Cogley's scorn for the demagogue. And those who saw the letter in its complete form in the *Chicago Catholic Worker* read the strongest Catholic attack on Coughlin up to that time.

Cogley wrote:

> followers of you have become Jew baiters and have quoted you in order to hold the threat of a pogrom over the Jew. It is your responsibility to set your followers straight . . .[since] anti-Semitism among Catholics is due to the inept untimely, stupidly construed study of Judaism you have devoted your-self to these last months.[16]

To further subdue the rising tide of anti-semitism among their coreligionists, the Chicago Catholic Workers helped organize the "Committee of Catholics to Fight Anti-Semitism". The formation of this group was conceived by Emmanuel Chapman, a Jewish convert to Catholicism and professor of philosophy at Fordham University He enlisted the aid of Dorothy Day, and together they attracted a group of people concerned over the deterioration of Catholic-Jewish relations. They published a paper called *Voice* which published censures of anti-Semitism by famous Catholics.[17] The paper also sent reporters to

---

[16]*Chicago Catholic Worker*, May, 1939. One of COughlin's biographers, Charles Tull, also quotes this letter from Cougley. Although he described it as the "best Catholic critique" of Coughlin, he called it a gentle criticism. Tull apparently read only the *Social Justice* version of the letter. The edited version hardle represented the enmity that existed between the Catholic Worker and Coughlin; Tull, *Father Coughlin*, pp. 208-209.

[17]Miller, *Harsh and Dreadful Love*, p.152.

Christian Front meetings to expose the group's activities.[18]

The Catholic Workers in Chicago formed a branch of the New York Committee in July 1939. They enlisted professors from Notre Dame and the University of Chicago to write articles for *Voice* and to serve on a free speakers bureau whose members talked to local school and parish groups. Ed Marciniak became permanent chairman of the group. He coordinated speaker appearances, wrote articles for *Voice* and prepared radio broadcasts which attacked anti-semitism.[19] From their headquarters in Chicago, the committee sent speakers and broadcasts throughout the Midwest, even to Coughlin's own city of Detroit. Ed Marciniak even went to Detroit and remembered in an interview nervously giving a speech there. Although their accomplishments were small, at least they provided some comfort to their Jewish brothers and sisters who were suffering through one of the greatest crises in their history.

Since Chicago never experienced the full onslaught of an organized Christian Front movement, many thought that the Catholic Worker reaction was an exageration of fact. Irate readers deluged their office with letters calling them "hypocritical Jew lovers", who "reached rash conclusions with little evidence." And members who sold the paper on the street suffered verbal and sometimes even physical abuse.[20]

------

[18]*Voice*, September, 1939; this issue described a Christian front meeting where a film was being shown. One part of the film showed a Jewish girl selling the leftist paper *Equality* on the street. This brought comments from the projectionist such as, "Look at that beak!" "Watch those kikes!" "Look at that dirty Communist Jew selling *Equality*!"

[19]Program of the committee as outlined in the *New York Times*, August 7, 1939.

[20]Miller,*Harsh and Dreadful Love*, p.152; Cogley, *Catholic America*, p.97.

The accusations of many were silenced on January 14, 1940, when they read in their morning papers that the Fedderal Bureau of Investigation had uncovered a plot by the Christian Front movement in New York to blow up the offices of the Communist *Daily Worker* also the offices of B'nai B'rith, steal arms and ammunition from the National Guard Armory, and eventually take over the government.[21] Even those who laughed at such fatuous plans, shuddered when they discovered that the head of the National Guard in New York sympathized with the Front's plan, as did many police captains who would have been expected to provide the first line of defense had such a coup been attempted.[22]

Coughlin suppported the Christian Front throughout their conspiracy trial, and after this final departure from reality he lost much of his following. Shortly after this episode, Coughlin withdrew from the public scene under threat of being defrocked by Archbishop Edward Mooney. Soon his crusade became a memory, but while the germ of anti-semitism spread by Coughlin had threatened to become a national epidemic, the Catholic Worker opposition reminded their Jewish friends that not all Catholics were willing to join the nativists' campaign and some were actually prepared to fight to prevent the atrocities against Jews in Europe from being repeated here.

The motivation for defense of the Jews in the thirties was the underlying raison d'etre of the Catholic Worker. Basic to the Worker philosophy was the desire to make moral values central to life. In the past, all systems had worked on some moral ontology, but in the industrial age, economic fact had taken precedence over all others.. "Value" had been substituted for "good". Political beliefs did not express

---

[21]*New York Times*, January 16, 1940; Ibid., May 3, 1940.

[22]*Chicago Tribune*, January 16, 1940.

moral persuasion, but rather economic point of view. The Catholic Worker's goal was the reconstruction of a moral tradition and to do this they became pioneers in the new liturgical reform movement emerging in the country.

Following the thought of the liturgist Virgil Michel, they hoped to promote a liturgy which involved the laity in active worship and which emphasized the ties that bound Christians and all humanity together. Such a liturgy, they believed, would make Catholics aware once again of the moral obligations they had to society. According to Michel, the liturgy of the Church provided Christians "with the divine model of social fellowship. It gives each member the inspiration of a personal growth. . . , and is itself the very source of all help by which man can achieve his highest development as a person and as a member of this fellowship."[23] In Europe the liturgical movement was an issue of abstract theological theory, but in this country Michel viewed it as a "solid foundation for the cooperative spirit of the Christian social order".

"Whether we thrill to the proposition or not", Cogley wrote, "by receiving Holy Communion [you] become one with the poor Negro charwoman in the rear of the church. . ., with the horny handed laborer in the coal mines [and] with the unwashed Russian peasant". There was a revolution inherent in going to mass Cogley concluded, since it "Demolishes all bariers . . . that separate man from his fellow man and raises obligations of social justice."[24]

Because of its social implications, this idea always remained important to Cogley, but liturgical reform never accomplished what its supporters had set out to do. The liturgists

---

[23]Virgil Michel, "Personality and Liturgy," *Oratre Fratres*, (February 19, 1939), p.159. This magazine which Michel edited until his death is the chief source of his ideas.

[24]*Chicago Catholic Worker* June 1940.

hoped to return Christian morality to the philosophic center of life. It was an appeal to a moral tradition centuries old, but ironically the conservatives in the church saw the movement as an attempt to replace traditional values with contemporary or transitory ones. On the contrary it was the conservatives who were content with the transvaluation of values which had taken Christian morality out of the heart of western value systems and placed it on the shelf as a curiosity. A latin mass at which one was an observer not a participant was symptomatic of the new weltänschauûng of the industrial age.

Throughout the forties and fifties the liturgical movement gained strength in Chicago among socially concerned Catholics. It became fundamental to the Christian Family Life movement and other groups which adopted a philosophy and spirit similar to that of the Catholic Worker. Finally in the 1960's Rome embraced the concept and it became a central issue of reform during the Vatican Council.

Many seeds were responsible for the final blossoming of liturgical reform, and in Chicago many of them were sown in the thirties by the Catholic Worker movement. In the December, 1939 edition of their paper, John Cogley announced a series of lectures on Church liturgy and social reform. Although the talks were free, those who wished to attend were asked to fill out an application. They made this requirement in order to be certain they would have an audience. The house on Blue Island Avenue was never as successful as its counterpart on Taylor Street in attracting people for conferences and discussions.

Their first lecture had almost been their last. A famous monk from a mendicant order had come to give a talk and only two people had come to hear him. In order to avoid embarrassment both for the speaker and themselves, the Workers asked some of their houseguests if they would attend the talk. Unlike many houses of refuge, the Catholic Worker never demanded attendance at an

LIBRARY ST. MARY'S COLLEGE

assembly before receiving a meal. Recognizing the plight of their young hosts, the men rubbed the spots off their cleanest shirts and skipped out the back door into the alley. A few minutes later they appeared at the front door, politely took their seats and listened to a discourse on a topic they neither understood nor cared to hear. Face being saved, the Workers resolved never to place themselves in that situation again.[25]

The announcement and the request for applications not only helped them avoid a similar accident, but it served, they soon discovered as a succesful ploy for attracting large crowds. "The place was filled to the rafters", O'Gara recalled, "There were people from all walks of life. . . a large number of college students, a couple of seminarians, some unemployed, and several social workers."[26]

These were exciting times for the people that ran the Catholic Worker house. With their plunge into social action, their soupline, and their newspaper, they confidently assured themselves that they were participating in the implementation of a new creation. As Andrew Greeley has pointed out, "In the late thirties in Chicago there began a series of experiments which would anticipate in amny respects the spirit and the teaching of the Vatican Council." These experiments, he pointed out, "would be imitated all over the United States and men who began them would become national figures and heroes to progressive Catholics all over the country."[27]

---

[25]*Chicago Catholic Worker*, January, 1940; Joan Smith O'Gara interview, James O'Gara interview, June 26, 1976, Rockville Center, New York.

[26]O'Gara interview;*Chicago Catholic Worker*, January 1940.

[27]Andrew Greeley, *The Catholic Experience: An Interpretation of the History of American Catholicism*(New York: Doubleday and Company, 1967), pp. 248-249.

LIBRARY ST. MARY'S COLLEGE

Another Catholic thinker wrote that as a student in the thirties in Chicago he and his friends formed quite a conscious subculture within American Catholicism. "We read, argued and acted as if the spirit of the ancient church supported us. We had our gods," he admitted, "and John Cogley was mine." Writing in the mid-sixties, when change for the better within the Church seemed imminent, Donald Costello, considering the activites of the Catholic Worker on Blue Island Avenue concluded, "the battles planned and fought so brilliantly by the Cogley's, Marciniak's and O'Gara's seem to be almost won."[28]

---

[28]Donald Costello, "The Chicago Ghetto" in Daniel Callahan ed., *Generation of a Third Eye* (New York: Sheed and Ward, 1965) pp. 62,67.

CHAPTER VI

LABOR

On Memorial Day, 1937, the crack of gunshots pierced the air outside the Republic Steel Mill. Ten workers died, and many more fell seriously wounded from the bullets and billyclubs which rained upon them that day. "Whom shall we blame for this horrible spectacle of violence?" Dorothy Day wondered. "Of course the police and the press place the blame on the strikers. But I have lived with these people", she wrote. "I have eaten with them and they are men and women like you and me, many of them never having been in a strike before." Some had even brought their children to the picket line that day. "It had been a supplicatory procession."[1]

A number of Catholic Workers had witnessed the fury that day. For almost a year prior to the Memorial Day violence, they had been helping the Steel Workers Organizing Committee (S.W.O.C.) unionize the employees of Republic Steel. During these early organizing days the Catholic Worker proved to be a valuable ally. Through rallies, worker discussion groups and pamphlets they explained to skeptical Catholic employees not only their right, but their obligation, to support good unions. The impact of a Catholic group supporting the cause of labor in an era when most union organizing was considered a Communist activity cannot be overemphasized. "Our presence caused quite a stir" Arthur Falls reported, "People could not get over a group in the name of Catholicism being interested in labor."[2]

When the long anticipated strike finally occurred, the Catholic Workers, carrying signs

---

[1] *Catholic Worker*, June 1937.

[2] Ibid.

which quoted the papal encyclicals, joined the picket lines. They also sat in "Sam's Place", a tavern at 113th and Green Bay Avenue which served as strike headquarters. In the rambling old building they fixed sandwiches and coffee and in other ways tried to maintain the morale of the workers who were caught up in the pressures of their ill-fated struggle with the steel industry.[3]

A few had even marched that warm Monday evening when the police, encouraged and fortified by an editorial in the *Chicago Tribune*, defended the property of Republic Steel by slaying the "Steel Strike Rioters" as they were described in the daily paper. [4] Police reported that shots which rang out from the direction of the crowd justified the killing of demonstrators, but John Cogley reported, "There were no arms [among the strikers] unless they were magically concealed on others who marched with us." A young boy at the strike headquarters told Cogley that his brother was on the picket line and his brother-in-law was a policeman on duty there. "It was a peculiar war" surmised Cogley, "in which brother is set against brother [sic]".[5]

"Where does the blame for oppression lie?" Dorothy Day questioned. "Shall we blame Tom Girdler of Republic Steel? Shall we blame only the police?" Could people ignore "the guilt of the press or the pulpit, or other agencies that have failed to raise up their voice in protest? We are all guilty," she asserted, "in as much as we have not protested such murder as occurred in Chicago, we are all guilty."

---

[3]as reported by Cogley, *Catholic Worker*, July 1937; and in his autobiography, *A Canterbury Tale*, p.13. Accounts of the strike are also related in interviews with Arthur Falls, Ed Marciniak, Tom Sullivan, and Monsignor John Hayes.

[4]*Chicago Tribune*, May 31, 1937.

[5]*Chicago Catholic Worker,* July, 1937.

The Catholic Workers, armed with a philosophy of Christian personalism, immersed themselves into the class conflicts of the thirties. They did not protest simply against the exploitation of workers or their oppression, but against the complete obliteration of human values which allowed such oppression of one class by another. "The capitalist system has forgotten the traditional Christian respect for the dignity of the individual", Ed Marciniak wrote in the *Chicago Catholic Worker*, "and modern society fails to appreciate the fact that Christ became man and by so doing ennobled human dignity."[6] Marciniak did not have to limit his censure to capitalism; every modern economic system had discarded any sense of "human dignity" as he called it. In the modern age all systems were based on power and economic strength. Coming from a Catholic tradition, he felt the need for a different basis for economic relationships and this sense was strengthened by his contact with the Catholic Worker. But the Worker lay outside the mainstream of American Catholicism in the 1930's. As John Cogley later pointed out, "with the emergence of the lace curtain Irish, the embourgeoisment of the Germans of the Middle West and the growing prosperity of the Italians, the Church's financial picture was bright" in the 1920's and thirties.[7] One of the casualties of prosperity was the loss of the spirit of community which had been nurtured in Christian Europe for thousands of years. With this loss came the disappearance of obligations to charity. "Although Catholic Social Action has been heralded and acclaimed with fervent fanfare", Cogley editorialized, "Real Catholic action never occurred, it was lost in long winded orations, speeches, press releases and pamphlets. The truth

---

[6]*Chicago Catholic Worker*, May 1939.

[7]John Cogley, *Catholic America* (New York: Dial Press, 1973), p. 80.

remained that very few Catholics really cared for the poor."[8]

It was these same Catholics, Ed Marciniak pointed out, who condemned poorer members of their faith for casting their lot with the Communists.[9] In the thirties the Communists made succesful inroads among working class Catholics. Although many sympathized with the Communists as a result of popular front political activity such as the "Free Ireland" movement, or their opposition to Nazi Germany, many more joined the ranks of the Communist party for their defense of the poor and the unemployed. Impoverished Catholics, as well as others, supported the *Daily Worker* which condemned the bishops of America in 1937 for "defending the rights of capital to suck profits from the undernourished bodies and growing minds of little children". They also agreed with the *Daily Worker* allegation that the "Catholic hierarchs are serving the brass god of Mammon"[10]

Marciniak believed that the Catholic attraction to the Communist Party was because among the Communists Catholics discovered a spirit of community that their own religion no longer possesed. "Sincere intelligent Communists are living in the drabbest neighborhoods among the neediest people," he pointed out, "while we Catholics sit in upholstered chairs announcing our great love for the poor." The Communists "were preaching Marxism to the poor", he chided,

---

[8]*Chicago Catholic Worker,*April, 1940.

[9]Ibid., November 1938.

[10]This particular condemnation occurred when the bishops opposed a child labor law because it would undermine the traditional authority of the family. Ralph Lord Roy, *Communism and the Churches*(New York: Harcourt, Brace and Company, 1960), p.132.

"while we Catholics talk Christianity over ban-
quet tables to ourselves."[11]
"We must go to the workers as one of them,"
Marciniak wrote, "Million dollar institutions in
the middle of slums will not help the worker, but
simple homes with simple tables, simple
hospitality and simple comradeship will." Marciniak told his fellow Catholics that "going to
the worker should be a matter of conscience for
all of us." The Church's position should be on
the side of the downtrodden. "When the
exploiters of human dignity can look to us for
condemnation regardless of how much they seem to
be pillars of the Church", and the exploited can
look to the Church for hope, then he affirmed,
"We will be going to the worker". Whether he had
done it consciously or not, Marciniak had
absorbed and succinctly summarized Peter Maurin's
philosophy of personal responsibilty. Although
modern society had shifted the burden of social
responsibility to institutions, Maurin believed
as his biogrpher Marc Ellis has pointed out, that
it was "worthwhile even salvific to care personally for those whom society had abandoned".
Herein lies the radicalism of the Worker movement, Ellis writes, for to demand personal
responsibility for the poor was to challenge the
person's and culture's perception of time and
progress.[12] For editorials such as Marciniak's,
the Catholic Worker has written itself into the
intellectual and social history of the American
Catholic Church. For at the precise moment that
a majority of Catholics were experiencing the
material benefits of American capitalism, the
Catholic Worker reminded bishops, priests and
laity alike that there were theological impedi-
ments to acquisitiveness and exploitation. And
while many Catholics were willing to embrace the

---

[11]*Chicago Catholic Worker*, November 1938.

[12]Marc Ellis *Peter Maurin: Prophet in the
Twentieth Century*(New York: Paulist Press, 1981),
p.170.

new morality of the "Christian businessman" as proclaimed by the Rotarian gospel, the *Catholic Worker* reminded them that Christ was a carpenter.

In the thirties a number of socially concerned Catholics voiced a concern over the rights of labor, but few groups emerged which could rival the the support given by the Chicago Catholic Worker to unions and union organizers. Many Catholic leaders disagreed over the direction their commitment to labor should take. These disagreements became especially acrid in the late thirties when the C.I.O. (Congress of Industrial Organization) launched its great organizing drive. Even Monsignor John Ryan, best known leader in American Catholic social action, questioned the desirability of a strong union, as historian David O'Brien has pointed out, "like other pioneers of American Social Catholicism, Ryan regarded co-operatives and voluntary profit sharing programs as more promising avenues to social justice than trade unions."[13]

Many important Catholic leders fell short of supporting the C.I.O. because certain aspects of their union activism lay counter to their Faith. Particularly troubling to many Catholics were the Sit-Down Strikes which offended their belief in a person's right to private property. The violence

---

[13]O'Brien, *American Catholics and Social Reform*, p.99. Ryans biographer, Francis Broderick,*Right Reverend New Dealer*(New York: Mac Millan and Company, 1963), does not agree with O'Brien. He states that the priest did not let his "distaste for real Communists affect his support [for unions], however it was a qualified approval and only came after he was pressured by a few leading bishops to make a statement condemning the CIO." Ryan's biographer fails to mention the frequency with which Ryan chastized the unions especially during the famous "Sit-Down" Strikes against General Motors. For Ryan's views on the Sit Down Strikes see: John A. Ryan, "The Sit Down Strike", *Ecclesiastical Review*(April, 1937): pp. 419-420.

emanatating from many strikes and the presence of
Communists on the strike lines also disturbed
many Catholics. In 1937, the bishops of the
United States, in a joint statement, warned labor
against the use of violence and coercion in union
activity and urged them to form joint bodies with
their employers to settle disputes. Bishop Lucey
of Texas was one of the few Catholic leaders who
did not support Catholic campaigns against
unionism. In fact, the crusade against communists in the unions particularly troubled
Lucey. Believing that this was a propaganda
device designed to turn people against unions,
Lucy declared that those who accused the unions
of "being filled with Communists" were "slander-
ing the working class." [14]

When the Chicago Catholic Workers decided to
support the C.I.O. in their city they pursued a
course quite different from their counterparts in
New York. Although Peter Maurtin applauded the
Sit Down strike as an example of Ghandi's effec-
tive non-violent protests , he viewed unionism
negatively.[15] Maurin believed that industrialism
had defined the worker as a mere commodity and
taken away his dignity as a partner in creation.
Unions he felt, by accepting this definition and

---

[14]Ralph Hunter ed. , *Our Bishops
Speak*(Milwaukee: Bruce Publishing Company, 1952),
pp. 98-101. Robert J. Lucey, "Labor in Recession," *Commonweal* 38 (May 6, 1938): p.47. For
an example of Catholic reaction to the sit down
strikes see Paul Blakely, "Labor Wages a Losing
Battle," *America*56 (February 6, 1937): pp. 417-
418; John Fichter, "What's Wrong With the Sit-
Down Strike?" *Catholic World* 145 (August 1937) :
pp.567-572.

[15]For Maurin's views on unions see Dorothy
Day, *Loaves and Fishes* (New York: Curtiss Books,
1972), pp.20-22.

merely arguing over the price of the comodity had
cooperated in this diminution of the worker.[16]

Maurin's views of unions became tempered by
his association with Dorothy Day. Her years as a
Socialist caused her to view the problems of
labor in terms of class conflict and therefore to
affirm and support the right and duty of working-
men to organize. "By himself", she wrote, "the
worker could do very little", therefore he had to
join in association with fellow workers to have
the strength to bargain collectively with
employers.[17] But it was obviously Maurin's
influence which caused her to conclude that
Catholic participation in a labor meeting should
be for the purpose of bringing the social teachings of the Church to the man on the street. The
great job of the Catholic Worker, she affirmed,
was to "reach the workers and bring them a
philosophy of labor, and speak to them of
Christian solidarity."[18]

In Chicago, the Catholic Workers were only
slightly influenced by Maurin's views on labor,
and they immersed themselves in the more practical task of organizing the industrial worker in
an A.F of L (American Federation of Labor) city.
To Marciniak , unionism was not a matter of
"wealth versus numbers" but rather a question of
"human solidarity". He did not dwell on Maurin's
vision of how things ought to be but rather dealt
with the reality of how things were. To Marciniak
good unionism provided protection against
exploitation of workers. Properly conceived,
unionism, he wrote, was "men joining together to
protect their human dignity". In Chicago the
Catholic Workers followed Marciniak's leadership

---

[16]For his theory of worker as artist and
partner in creation, Maurin leans quite heavily
on Eric Gill. See Eric Gill,*It All Goes Together*
(New York: Devin Adair, 1944).

[17]*Catholic Worker*, September 1937.

[18]Ibid., January 1939.

on this issue and urged Catholics to join unions in order to exert a positive Christian influence on them. Without an influence which would emphasize human solidarity, Marciniak feared the labor would set up an "aristocracy within its ranks" which would remain "indifferent to humbler, unskilled workers," and the primary goal of human dignity would be lost.[19]

Marciniak believed that the future of American labor lay in the "C.I.O. or at least in the principle of industrial organization." It troubled him that there were few Catholic leaders in this union and that Catholics seemed willing to let the Communists have a free rein in industrial unionism. He urged the formation of a group of Catholics as dedicated as the Communists, who would join in "on the inside fighting . . . for a stronger and better labor movement." It was Marciniak's beliefs and energy which brought the Catholic Worker into Chicago's organized labor movement in the thirties.

Chicago had traditionally been a craft union city. Industrial organization as proposed by the C.I.O. had struggled and what success they had achieved was due to aid given them by the American Federation of Labor, a craft union. Unlike most cities, Chicago witnessed close cooperation between C.I.O. and A.F of L leadership and among the rank and file. But this relationship was severed abruptly in 1937, by an order from A.F of L president William Green. It was a sad annulment in Chicago, but the C.I.O. was growing rapidly and rather than dwell on past relationships they sought new allies.[20]

One of their important new allies in Chicago was the Catholic Church. Symbolically, the Church played an important role by having the

---

[19]*Chicago Catholic Worker*, March 1940.

[20]Barbara Newell, *Chicago and the Labor Movement: Metropolitan Unionism in the 1930s* (Urbana: University of Illinois Press, 1961), pp. 182-184.

popular Bernard Sheil greet John L. Lewis when he came to town, or by publishing quotations from papal encyclicals which urged Catholics to support unions. Cardinal Mundelein also supported Saul Alinsky's community organizing activities in the Back of the Yards neighborhoods, the poor areas in which the packinghouse workers lived.[21] More important than this hierarchical support however was the grass roots work of organizing, propagandizing and when necessary manning picket lines. It was in these activities that the Catholic Worker made its greatest contribution to the labor movement in Chicago.

Before the outbreak of the war, the C.I.O., suffering from its tragic defeat at the hands of Republic Steel, could count very few victories for its cause. two notable exceptions, however, the meatpackers union and the newspaper guild, gave the C.I.O. hope of better days to come. The Chicago Catholic Worker gave important help in both these drives and their assistance was an important factor in the C.I.O.'s success.

By 1938, most of the newspaper industry had been organized. Printers, truck drivers and maintenance men all enjoyed comfortable contracts with the large newspaper chains throughout the country. The exception to this rule was the newspaper writer. The depression had been particularly hard on the writers. There were a number of reasons for their lack of organization and low pay. The most frequently cited cause was that newspaper writers were too dedicated, too romantically inclined and too independent for

---

[21]Edward Kantowicz, *Corporation Sole: Cardinal Mundelein and Chicago Catholicism* (South Bend: University of Notre Dame Press, 1983), pp.193-196; Newell, *Chicago Labor Movement*, pp.244-245.

union organization. [22] Although the image of the image of the dedicated reporter fullfilling the public's need to be informed and indifferent to his material condition may have been a true one, other factors caused their poor economic circumstances.

The most obvious cause for their lack of organization was the surplus of their product. Every year, thousands of college graduates eager to begin a writing career descended on the large newspapers. Taking advantage of these would-be Hemingways, the papers hired and fired reporters rapidly causing a heavy turnover which eliminated job security and prevented the stability necessary for union organizing.[23] Some inroads were made by the Newspaper Guild, which had been organized by Heywood Broun in 1934, but for the most part this union remained a fragmented one, with some strength on the local level, but nationally wracked by dissension.[24] Of the five daily newspapers in Chicago in 1938, besides the mildly pro-labor *Times*, only the two Hearst papers had a large number of Guild writers.[25]

In January, 1938 the Guild protested to the Hearst management when Emmanuel Levi, the new publisher, began a series of economy moves which resulted in mass dismissals of writers. In a

---

[22]For example, J. Raymond Walsh, Harvard economist and C.I. O. histoprian held this opinion. See Walsh, *CIO*, (New York: Viking Press), also the A.F.of L.'s *Federation News*, September 2, 1935, expressed a similar opinion.

[23]Newell, *Chicago Labor Movement*, p. 187.

[24]Benjamine Stolberg, *The Story of the CIO* (New York: Viking Press, 1938), pp.250-252.

[25]*The Guild Reporter*, February 1, 1937 listed newspaper writer membership in Chicago as follows: *The Chicago American*, 97 of 124; *Herald Examiner,* 113 of 129;*Times*, 93 0f 108;*Daily News*, 23 of 135;*The Tribune*, 3 of 135.

late evening bargaining session the Guild
extracted an agreement from Levi not to dismiss
any more workers without consulting the union.
In December 1938, after numerous instances proved
that the publisher was ignoring the agreement,
the Newspaper Guild called a strike.[26]
      The action began futilely. Other unions in
the industry sent letters of sympathy to the
Guild, but they continued to honor their contracts with the Hearst papers.[27] The only noticeable result of the strike action against the two
papers was that they were forced to combine into
one publication, *The Chicago Herald-American*, and
management had to take over reporting assignments. The publishers chose to ignore the
strikers and the rest of the industry did
likewise, as no news of the strike appeared in
any of Chicago's daily newspapers. Since the
radio stations also respected the blackout, the
strikers were stripped of their only means of
victory, favorable propaganda.
      As the strike began, the Guild searched for
allies and found few. The C.I.O., with whom they
were affiliated, was too weak and the A.F. of L
remained indifferent if not antagonistic to the
upstart union. [28] The craft union represented
other trades in the newspaper industry and the
Guild strike threatened the security of these
workers. Consequently, during the strike the A.F.
of L eventually came down on the side of management, and dealt a serious blow to the Guild.
Before the strike was many days old, the A.F.of
L's *Federation News,* declared that the strike
was "not a labor dispute. . . but rather a fight

---

[26]*Guild Strike News*, January   1939;*The
Chicago Catholic Worker,*February 1939.

[27]*Guild-Hearst Strike News,*January 1938;
Chicago Catholic Worker, February 1939; Newell,
Chicago Labor Movement, p.189.

[28]Newell, *Chicago Labor Movement,*p. 189;
Stolbert, *C.I.O.* p. 250.

by Communists against a newspaper because of its determined opposition to Communism."[29]

On the national level the Guild had been tainted by this accusation before, and its enemies in Chicago exploited the controversy. For this reason support from a Catholic group became significant. Bishop Sheil supported the strike as well as the Archdiocese's official publication, *New World* which reported the progress of the strike in its first weeks.[30] In addition, Monsignor Reynold Hillenbrand, director of the seminary, lent his support to the strikers telling them, "The Catholic Church is behind you one hundred per cent." The Guild took advantage of these endorsements by announcing "Catholics Support Strike" in a headline of their paper, *The Guild-Hearst Strike News.*[31]

In addition to the moral and symbolic support received from Church leaders the Guild also recieved strong grass-roots support from the Chicago Catholic Workers. Joe Carroll, a member of the Guild's organizing committee, wrote to the Catholic Workers and requested their support. Aware that the "Catholic Worker had helped other unions in the past," he asked for their support knowing "the prestige of your name supporting the

---

[29]*Federation News,* December 15, 1938.

[30]*Guild-Hearst Strike News,* January 1939;*Chicago Catholic*

[31] Worker,Jauary, 1939; Edward Kantowicz, *Corporation Sole: Cardinal Mundelein and Chicago Catholicism* (South Bend: Notre Dame Press, 1983), pp.196-97; According to Monsignor John Hayes who played an important part in the strike , when Heywood Broun spoke at a Guild rally he pointed out that the only coverage the strike received was in the Catholic press. He thanked the editors of both the *New World* and the *Chicago Catholic Worker* for their fair coverage of the strike, Hayes interview.

Guild would be invaluable pressure in winning our demands."[32]

When the strike began, the Catholic Workers gave their full support. They joined picket lines, mimeographed pamphlets, contributed sandwiches and coffee and took part in all the jobs necessary to wage a long strike.[33] The November issue of the *Chicago Catholic Worker* reported that one of their members, Harry Read, had been arrested for distributing pamphlets outside the offices of the *Hearst American*. Read was acquitted, the *Worker* reported, "but the sentencewas appealed by the Hearst lawyers forcing Read to incur further expense to defend himself." The Catholic Workers made another important contribution to the strike with their newspaper. Since the capitalist press in the city had chosen to ignore the strike, the Guild had been forced to print a paper of its own which put an extra strain on meager resources. Beginning with their January 1939, issue however, the *Chicago Catholic Worker* provided complete coverage of the strike and expanded their circulation. The paper outlined the Guild's demands, appealed for funds for them and exposed the use of thugs and gangsters by the Hearst Company to intimidate the writers.

The use of a Catholic publication to report strike news was especially helpful in defusing a potentially embarassing situation for both the strikers and a Catholic bishop. Several months before the strike, Bishop Sheil had written a series of articles on Youth in Chicago. During the strike The *Herald-American* printed these articles making Sheil appear to be a strike breaker and supporter of the newspaper. Such support would have been an important propaganda weapon for the Hearst paper since at the beginning of the strike Sheil had influenced Catholic opinion by publicly suypporting the strike. To many people such a turnabout by Sheil

---

[32]*Guild-Hearst Strike News*, January 1939.

[33]*Chicago Catholic Worker*, June 1938.

would mean that the union must be making unfair demands on the publishers.

The Catholic Workers as well as the Guild members were incensed by the bishop's apparent turnabout, and in an open letter which appeared on the front page of the *Chicago Catholic Worker,* John Cogley chided the bishop for supporting the capitalist press. Chastising bishops publicly was not something lay Catholics normally did in the 1930's but Cogley and his fellow Catholic Workers were more bound by their own sense of mission than by tradition. Sheil called Cogley down to his office on Wabash Avenue and explained to the young editor that he had written the articles long before the strike broke out and that his name was being exploited by the Hearst Company.[34]

In the next issue of the *Chicago Catholic Worker* an open letter from Sheil appeared stating that his name had been used deceptively by the Hearst paper and that he fully supported the efforts and demands of the striking Guild members.[35] The Hearst response was to buy a full page advertisement in the *New World* to explain their position on the strike, but the value of this was diminished significantly by the circulation of Sheil's letter by the Catholic Worker.[36]

When the strike finally ended in the Fall of 1939, the results may hardly have seemed worth the suffering of the long struggle. All the Guild achieved was a face saving compromise. But

---

[34]A picture of Catholic Workers at the strike headquarters and a story on Catholic aid during the strike appeared in the *Guild-Hearst Strike News*, January 1939.

[35]*Chicago Catholic Worker*, March 1939; an account of this episode also appears in Cogley's obituary written by Tom Sullivan for the New York *Catholic Worker,* June 1976.

[36]*Chicago Catholic Worker*, March 1939;Neil Betten, "Urban Catholicism and Industrial Reform," *Thought* (Fall, 1969): p. 440.

the union had won recognition from the Hearst
enterprises and the Catholic Worker became known
as an important grass roots ally in labor organization. Following the Guild-Hearst strike, other
union organizers recognized the significance of
the Catholic Workers' support and through their
contributions they helped introduce the word
"Catholic" into the history of industrial
unionism in Chicago.

CHAPTER VII

INDUSTRIAL UNIONISM

Another labor organizer who sought help from the Catholic Worker was Van Bittner, chairman of both the Steel Workers, and the Packinghouse Workers Organizing Committees. In the difficult days of industrial union organizing in the thirties, the Catholic Worker was an important ally. As Ed Marciniak pointed out most Catholic laborers remained suspicious of unions and held attitudes toward unionism "shaped by the capitalist press." Cardinal Mundelein and Bishop Sheil supported the unions efforts in Chicago but in the struggle to organize meat packers, more than good wishes and supportive words were necessary.[1]

In Chicago an important, and sometimes permanent, stopping place for many Catholic immigrants was the stockyards. Before the turn of the century, cleaning and preparing meat had been an honorable trade, but this craft also, fell victim to the rationalizations of industrial order. By 1890 the assembly line, or rather the disassembly line, had been introduced to the meat packing business. From that time on, all that was needed to be a meat packer was a strong back and the ability to do repetitive tasks. A laborer could spend his entire day for months at a time, slicing the jowls off hogs as their carcasses were drawn past him on a moving chain.[2]

---

[1]Kantowicz, *Corporation Sole*, pp.193-195; also Neil Betten, *Catholic Activism and the Industrial Worker* (Gainesville: University of Florida Press, 1976), p.123.

[2]Alma Herbst, *The Negro in the Slaughtering and Meat Packing Industry* (Boston: Houghton Mifflin, 1931), provides an interesting picture of this industry in her introduction.

After putting in nine very chilly hours at the plant, life was little better at home for the worker. His family lived in a dismal area called "The Back of the Yards". Houses were squalid frame buildings of varying heights. They were divided into family dwellling units with as many as twelve people living in one small house. All of the houses had running water, but there was usually only one toilet set in the hall between two housing units. Bath tubs were scarce; over ninety percent were without them.[3] Despite their terrible conditions of work and living, the inhabitants of the Back of the Yards remained unorganized against this economic and spiritual oppression. As Saul Alinsky pointed out, the packers froze and suffered side by side in the factories, but on the streets they hardly spoke to one another. Even though most were Catholic all came from diverse European traditions. Even the priests of the neighborhood hardly greeted each other.[4] A number of strikes had been attempted, but the industry, taking advantage of the division among the people and strikebreakers, always defeated the workers. In the thirties the colossal task of organizing was undertaken by the C.I.O., and among the pioneers in this effort were Ed Marciniak and Al Reser of the Chicago Catholic Worker. Father John Hayes, the spiritual director of the Catholic Worker also went down to the stockyards frequently. Wearing his Roman collar he repeated to thhe workers over and over, "The Catholic Church is behind you in your effort to demand a living wage".[5] It was the first time that these immigrants had heard unionism defended by the Catholic Church and it

---

[3]Ed Skillin, "Back of the Stockyards," *Commonweal* 33 (November 29, 1940): p.143.

[4]Saul Alinsky, *Reveille for Radicals* (New York: Vintage Books, 1969), p.80.

[5]*Catholic Worker,* April 1937; Marciniak interview; Hayes interview.

became an important help for the C.I.O. in their organizing drive.

Bittner faced three major problems in organizing the meatpackers and help from the Catholic Worker helped minimize all three of them.[6] First of all the immigrants carried with them a prejudice against unions from Europe where unions were generally more political and strongly anti-clerical. Although many immigrants might have been less than fervent in their homelands, in America they clung to the Church which maintained at least a semblance of the culture they had left behind, and they were suspicious of any threats to this cultural shelter. These fears were greatly diminished by Catholic Worker pamphlets and reassurances by Catholic clergy. It was one thing for a bishop to advocate unions in a pastoral letter it was quite another to see a priest, such as Father Hayes, in his collar distributing union information. Bittner also faced the difficulty of unifying a group composed of divergent backgrounds, but religion did provide a common ground and rhetoric and the Catholic Worker helped Bittner exploit it. As Alinsky pointed out, Catholicism, which can emphasize diverse ethnic and cultural backgrounds, divided workers, but the Catholic Worker theology emphasized the unity of all Christians in the Mystical Body of Christ. Finally, Bittner had to overcome the powerful propaganda and influence of an industry dominated by corporate giants. By claiming the support of the Catholic Church, Bittner had the power of a giant on his side also.

Bittner was also helped by the *Chicago Catholic Worker* which published articles revealing the sordid working and living conditions of the packers. Many of these editions found their way into the hands of middle class Catholics who normally would not have a "labor" paper in their homes. In one edition they printed an interview

---

[6]These problems are outlined by Newell, *Chicago Labor Movement*, p.152.

with Frank Mc Carthy of the Packinghouse Workers
Organizing Committee (P.W.O.C.) which outlined
the goals and explained the purpose of the union.
Some members of the Catholic Worker also went to
the meat factories, obtained jobs and gave first
hand reports on conditions in the factories. The
nuns of an exclusive women's college on the North
Shore were surprised (some appalled) when they
learned that one of their students had spent her
summer working in a meat packing plant. June
Gardner reported in the *Chicago Catholic Worker*
on the bonus system used at Swifts which forced
employees into dangerous competition with one
another. "One woman's hand was stabbed by a fork
of another trying to get lean pieces of pork to
trim", she reported. She also commented that
there was "a noticeable absence of Negroes any-
where except in the most unskilled jobs."[7]
    The efforts of the Catholic Worker and the
P.W.O.C. had a successful culmination in the summer of 1939. After two years of organizing, the
P.W.O.C. held its first national convention. This
meeting witnessed the first public sanction by
the Catholic hierarchy of the C.I.O. organizing
attempts in Chicago.[8] The real significance of
the rally that day at the Chicago Coliseum was
not the appearance and speech of John L. Lewis,
but rather the drama which unfolded when Bishop
Sheil presented a militant defense of labor's
right to organize , and urged workers to close
ranks behind the C.I.O.[9]
    Aware of the impact that the bishops speech
would have on the C.I.O.'s organizing drive in
the Chicago, both the A.F.of L. and the remaining

---

[7]*Chicago Catholic Worker,*August 1941; Marciniak interview.

[8]Newell, *Chicago Labor Movement,*pp.167-168;
Kantowicz, *Corporation Sole*, p.196; *Chicago Daily
News*, July 12, 1939; *Chicago Tribune* July 17,
1939.

[9]*Commonweal* 30 (July 28, 1939).

unorganized industries tried to dissuade him. Before appearing, Sheil had been asked publicly by the Hearst papers, The Chicago Federation of Labor and a representative of the meat packing industries to forego the convention. The A.F. of L.'s *Federation News* stated that the appearance of Bishop Sheil was unfortunate for it dragged the Church into a situaiton where it did not belong and it made the issue of union organizing a political (Sheil was a strong supporter of President Roosevelt) rather than an economic question.[10] "Usually the bishops have avoided participation in controversial political and economic movements", sniffed the *Chicago Tribune*.[11]

A day before the rally a P.W.O.C. organizer was shot and seriously wounded, and Sheil also received an anonymous threat on his life, but he remained steadfast. "It is may duty as a priest of God, he declared, "to state clearly and briefly the position that has been expressed by our Pope on matters affecting the economic and social welfare of society."[12] Heartened by the prelate's support, and the successful summer of organizing, the meatpackers authorized their leaders to call a strike if recognition demands were not met. Two months after the convention, in a surprise reaction, the meat industry recognized the Packinghouse Workers Union and accepted their demands.[13]

Unlike the Catholic Worker in New York, the Chicago group became strong advocates of industrial unionism. They viewed reform within the context of modern industrialism, and therefore did not share Peter Maurin's rejection of the

---

[10]*Federation News*, August 5, 1939.

[11]*Chicago Tribune*, July 17, 1939.

[12]*Commonweal* 30 (July 28, 1939).

[13]Milton Derber and Edwin Young, *Labor and the New Deal* (Madison: University of Wisconsin Press, 1957), p. 298.

industrial order. A similar rebuff of Maurin's idea occurred in New York where John Cort and Martin Wersing founded the Association of Catholic Trade Unionists at the Catholic Worker house there in 1937. Cort explained that the purpose of this group was "to build an organization of Catholic men and women who were at the same time active members of the established C.I. O., A.F. of L. or independent unions."[14]

In the Fall of 1938 a branch of the A.C.T.U. was established in Chicago at the Catholic Worker house. Ed Marciniak supported the A.C.T.U. because he saw it as a means of educating Catholic workers so they might have an influential voice within their unions, and under Catholic Worker and A.C.T.U. auspices the first Catholic labor schools were established in Chicago at the Blue Island Avenue house of hospitality.[15] Included in the curriculum were courses designed to give workers ability to take leadership roles within their respective unions. Included were courses on parliamentary procedure, collective bargaining and the social teachings of the Church. Through the effort of Father John Hayes and the influence of Monsignor Reynold Hillenbrand, the Archdiocese also opened four more labor schools in various parts of the city.[16]

It would be too facile to say that the Catholic Worker led the Archdiocese into the labor movement. There existed in Chicago in the late thirties a relationship between laity and clergy that would be difficult to imitate in any

----

[14]John Cort, "Catholics in Trade Unions," *Commonweal* 30 (May 5, 1939):pp 34-36. For a good overview of the A.C.T.U. see Neil Betten, *Catholic Activism and the Industrial Worker*, pp.125-145.

[15]*Chicago Catholic Worker*, July 1938.

[16]Kantowicz, *Corporation Sole*, p.201; Cort, "Catholics in Trade Unions", p.35; *New World*, March 19, 1938.

other Catholic community in America. Under the influence of Hillenbrand, Hayes, and a few others such as Father Cantwell, the director of CISCA, there existed in Chicago a group of young Catholic intellectuals in the late thirties whose motivation was the injection of Catholic social thought into the challenges of their time. The Catholic Worker provided much of the intellectual fodder for this group which would not have been satisfied with cliches on do-goodism. For this reason it was embraced and nurtured in Chicago by clerical and lay activists. Whereas the New York Catholic Worker always operated on the periphery of the official Church, the Chicago Worker was a product of the activism inherent in the liberal atmosphere of the Archdiocese under the leadership of Cardinal Mundelein.[17]

One of the schools which met at St. Mary Seminary in Mundelein was designed specifically for priests. It taught clerics how to approach the question of unionism with their parishioners and how to encourage them to join and support unions.[18] In the decades that followed the Archdiocese embraced this loose association of learning centers and formed the Sheil School of Social Studies, which became a center for Catholic social action in the forties and fifties.[19]

The most significant contribution made by the A.C.T.U. was the assistance it gave to the

---

[17]Mundelein's biographer, Edward Kantowicz, wrote that the Cardinal, a friend of President Roosevelt, followed the Rooseveltian tactic of allowing "a riot of experimentation" to go on with his sanction; *Corporation Sole*, p.202.

[18]*Chicago Catholic Worker*, July 1938; Newell, *Chicago Labor Movement*, p.244; Cogley, *Catholic America*, pp.92-93; O'Brien, *Catholics and Reform*, pp.112-113.

[19]Kantowicz, *Corporation Sole, pp.191-192;* Andrew Greely, *The Catholic Experience*, pp.254-256.

C.I.O. in attracting large numbers of Catholics
into the union. More than one historian has concluded that without A.C.T.U. propaganda and
instruction on the social teaching of the Church,
most Catholics would have remained outside of
organized unions in the 1930's.[20]
After the war began and unions became more
powerful, the A.C.T.U. became embroiled in the
factionalism which plagued the C.I.O. in the
forties. The A.C.T.U. drifted away from the
Catholic Worker and in Chicago it became defunct.
The A.C.T.U. began to be dominated by right wing
union members intent on driving Communists and
left wing unionism from power. One labor historian, Art Preis, described the A.C.T.U. as the
most aggressive force withn unionism in the
struggle against the Communists. This agency, he
discovered "put a great deal of pressure on
Catholic unionists like Phillip Murray and
incited the most reactionary tendencies inside
the C.I.O. to wage a witch hunt against the Communists." For this reason, despite the important
work of organizing done in the thirties the
legacy of the A.C.T.U. is that it was a reactionary faction within the C.I.O. which spearheaded
the anti-Communist drive.[21] Ed Marciniak, probably the most involved of Catholic labor leaders
in Chicago, also became disillusioned with the
direction the A.C.T.U. took in the forties. In a
letter to John Cort, the president of the Union,
he complained that union leaders ought to
"emphasize the individual member's own
responsibility as a member of his union, rather
than as a member of a faction." He feared that

---

[20]For example, Max Kampelmen, *The Communist
Party vs. The CIO*(New York: Frederick Praeger
Inc., 1957), p.152; Betten, *Catholic Activism and
the Industrial Worker*, pp.125, 144-145.

[21]Art Preis, *Labor's Giant Step*(New York:
Pioneer Publishers, 1964), p.336; Betten,
Catholic Activism and the Industrial Worker,
pp.144-145.

"some Catholics [namely A.C.T.U. members] lost
perspective of the main job, which is the reform
of the economic and social system." Instead,
they had thrown their weight behind a "let's
clean out the labor movement campaign."[22]
Despite its radical origins in the thirties, by
the 1940's the A.C.T.U. had become a reformist
organization working within the established
framework. In a final estimation of the A.C.T.U.
Dorothy Day who was leaning more toward the
decentralist idea of Peter Maurin, stated that
"all they [A.C.T.U.] want is a share in the profits." Unlike the Catholic Worker they were not
interested in the "ownership and decentralization
of the physical business of facotries and production and the decentralization of control by
widespread ownership."[23] Cort, for his part,
felt that decentralization was unrealistic. The
industrial revolution and its implications could
not be repealed, and any effort to do so, he
maintained, would be anachronistic. In *Commonweal*
he wrote that there was not any "aid and comfort
for anarchism in the wisdom of the Church,
despite the extended and often eloquent efforts
of the Catholic Worker movement to find such aid
and comfort."[24]

Philosophically, the Chicago Catholic Worker
remained between the two positions establshed by
Cort on one hand and Dorothy Day on the other.
Marciniak rejected Cort's goal to dominate union
policy. He emphasized the individual
responsibility inherent in the personalist
philosophy of the Catholic Worker. He felt that
the factionalism which ran rampant in the C.I.O.

---

[22]Marciniak to Cort, February 4, 1950, (Marciniak papers).

[23]*Catholic Worker,* February 1949.

[24]John Cort, "The Charms of Anarchism", *Commonweal* 57 (November 14, 1952): p.140.

diminished the significance of the individual.[25] On the other hand, Marciniak, as well as a number of other Catholic Workers, rejected Peter Maurin's views on unions. Maurin viewed collective bargaining and unionism as an immediate necessity, but a transitory one. Rather than building good unions, Maurin felt more energy should be expended educating the worker away from the idea of a centralized, highly depersonalized, industrial society. Collective bargaining, he felt, ought to provide a breathing spell for the indoctrination of workers in the idea of "personalist democracy". Most labor historians who record the labor activities of the Catholic Worker movement in the thirties and forties have dismissed Maurin's ideas as the attempt to resurrect the medieval corporate idea of the Church.[26] They call Maurin a dreamer who was not dealing with the real world. However time continues to vindicate Maurin. He increasingly can be put in the context of a Ghandi, who said "our goal should not be mass production but rather production by the masses" or the noted British economist E.F. Schumaker who has documented the failure of the modern industrial structure and advocates a revamping of the system on a more manageable scale. At one time Maurin was called a dreamer who lived in a fantasy world. But as the century comes to a close, it seems that the mythology of the nineteenth and twentieth centuries which denied fundamental human relationships and viewed both the land and the people on it as resources to be exploited, has become a very costly fantasy.

Although Maurin felt that a decentralized economy could eventually redeem modern urban life, he believed his vision of personalized democracy could be realized more easily in a

---

[25]Ed Marciniak, "Catholic Social Doctrine and the Layman," *America* 100 (February 7, 1959).

[26]For example Betten, *Catholic Activism and the Industrial Worker*, p. 57.

rural environment. Basically, his communal farming ideas were similar to others of the nineteenth and twentieth centuries who looked to the
land as a refuge from the plight of the city.
But in Maurin's scheme, the concept became pecu-
liarly Catholic. As Dorothy Day wrote, "Peter
wanted to restore the communal aspect of
Christianity". He wanted the Catholic Worker to
be "rich in voluntary poverty, free to devote
itself to the works of mercy." He wanted farms
where "families could live and work together. . .
where there could be a certain amount of common
life, work for all, and a school where all could
learn to work."

"On a farm" Maurin felt, there existed a way
of life "in which all the variety,
responsibility, [and] integrity of action which
are removed from the usual existence of the wage
earner are restored to him so that he can once
again function as a human being rather than as a
machine minder." Maurin also believed that
Catholic philosophy was particularly appropriate
for a communal life. Catholics alone he said,
"understand that while the family is the primary
social unit, the community comes next. And there
is no sound and enduring community where all its
members are not substantially of one mind in matters of the spirit, that is to say of religion".[27]

The farming commune idea remained alien to
most members of the Chicago Catholic Worker.
They accepted the Worker's ideas of personalism
and communal obligation, but they felt that these
ideas must be worked out in an urban environment
where most of humanity lived. There was,
however, a small group at the Catholic Worker who
became impressed with Maurin's idea of a farming
commune. Catherine Reser, one such enthusiast,
writing an article for the *Chicago Catholic
Worker*, explained that "the farming program is an
integral part of the movement", She feared that

---

[27]Dorothy Day, *Loaves and Fishes* pp. 42-
44,53.

the breadline and the shelter had overwhelmed the rural dimension of the movement, but she hoped that in the "near future the farming commune will become the distinguishing feature of the Catholic Worker." With a farm she wrote, "We hope to demonstrate a way of life in which men could assume personal responsibility for their economic salvation." [28]

Those interested in the farm commune began to hold discussions at the Worker house and Catherine Reser wrote long articles on farming which appeared each month in the paper. In the summer of 1940 they were able to put theory to practice. A Catholic woman, impressed with their articles and apparent determination to create a farming experiment, donated anonymously one hundred twenty acres of land in northern Minnesota to the Chicago Catholic Workers. [29]

After moving to the farm, the Catholic communists soon discovered that there was more to farming than theorizing and discussing the benefits of rural life. Tom Sullivan recalled that the city-raised Workers were ill-prepared for their farming experiment. He remembered visiting the farm and when they should have been getting up to milk the cow, they were just going to bed after a long night's discussion. Even if the Workers had been experienced farmers, they would have been hard pressed to make the rugged and rocky terrain of northern Minnesota fruitful. Consequently, the Catholic Worker farm remained a liability. The house in the city continued to send food to the one in the country when all along the ooposite had been planned. [30] To the disappointment of few, the farming commune ended shortly after the war began when the draft board sent Marty Paul, the leader of the farming expe-

---

[28] *Chicago Catholic Worker*, March 1939.

[29] Ibid., May, 1939

[30] Sullivan interview.

riment to a conscientious objectors camp in New Hampshire.[31]

While the farm experiment was being carried out in Minnesota, the character of the house on Blue Island Avenue was changing. An older group of men began replacing the younger ones who were rushing back to the numerous factory jobs becoming available. As the demons in Europe became more distinguishable, Americans began to see more clearly the need to join in the conflict or at least to lend their resources. Domestic quarrels were quickly forgotten, and arm in arm workers and capitalists joined together to create an "Arsenal for Democracy". Forgetting their differences, Americans put aside questions of social reform and found community once again in an overseas campaign.

Apparently the need to defend labor against the harsh pulsations of capitalism had disappeared. Workers were earning large salaries, and the suffering of the depression was quickly becoming a distant memory. Nevertheless, the Catholic Workers still protested the evils of a system which continued to oppress workers if not in poverty, in other more subtle ways. A young mechanic visited Ed Marciniak and told him about injuries he had sustained on the job. "They talk about human beings [at the factory] as if they were broken tractors" Marciniak protested. But "that is the spirit of industry", he complained, "especially in time of war." Pointing out that the subordination of the human spirit to the material was a root cause of war, he asked the obvious: "when a lost worker is only a lost investment, what will happen when the situation changes and it becomes profitable to take a chance losing a worker?" But then, he added, "a fellow does not have to go overseas to become a

---

[31]Marty Paul interview. Paul wrote a diary of his experience on the Minnesota farm. Excerpts appear in his article "Diary of a Romantic Agrarian," *Commonweal* 57 (January 2, 1953): pp.327-30.

war victim, a steel mill can destroy him just as well." But "who cares?", he complained, "the money's rolling in, there's enough to pay for the flowers."[32]

While joining workers in their struggle in the thirties, the Catholic activists of Chicago hoped to integrate their own Christian views of social solidarity into the labor movement. They hoped as Peter Maurin had said to go to the worker to:

> tell the worker
> what is wrong
> with things as they are.
> [and] tell the worker
> how a path can be made
> from things as they are
> to things as they should be.

The Catholic Workers wanted to share a vision of the world that transcended the state as a basis of human solidarity. But as the war approached and workers rallied around their country's cause, the Catholic Workers watched their image of community disintegrate.

---

[32]*Chicago Catholic Worker*, October 1940.

CHAPTER VIII

PACIFISM

On a winter evening in 1941, John Cogley and a few of his friends gathered in his room to listen to some records of old songs from the World War. It struck him how different the music from that era had been. The tunes revealed an "air of gaiety" he felt which "was lost midst so much tragedy of the recent past". His generation which had just begun to regain their equilibrium after a decade of economic catastrophe, now found themselves bracing for a world war. It was understandable why Cogley and his friends preferred the melancholic strains of "The Last Time I Saw Paris" to the bravura of "Over There!"

The war in Europe had made the normal tensions around the Catholic Worker house even more trying. Normally disruptions came from outsiders such as the "guest" who objected to sleeping in the same room with blacks, whom Cogley told "Well you can always check in at the Drake!" But in 1941 dissension came increasingly from insiders whose objections could not be handled as glibly.

Although the Catholic Worker had been consistently pacifist since its inception, there were those who felt that in light of the horrors taking place in Europe that pacifism ought to be reconsidered, or at least clarified. It became an issue that struck to the core of the personalist philosophy of the Worker movement and it was a question which strained emotion as well as intellect. Often, casual conversations erupted into seering arguments inflicting wounds that never healed. When America finally did enter the Second World War, it marked the saddest and most disruptive chapter in the history of the Catholic Worker. In a very real sense the movement was one of the casualities of the war and although the wounds were not mortal, they caused serious mutations. And when the war ended there were many who had called themselves Catholic Workers in the thirties who would never claim that title again. Nowhere is the pain of this struggle more clearly depicted than in the story of the Chicago Catholic Worker.

In its short history the New York Catholic Worker had attracted a number of followers who would not have accepted Catholicism on any other terms. They were converts to the Catholic Worker but not to the faith which provided its philosophy. This characteristic did not however typify the Chicago Workers. Those who were part of the movement there were thoroughly Catholic even before they had heard of the movement, in fact, it was through there connection with the new wave of Catholic reform groups that people like Cogley, Marciniak , O'Gara and others learned of the Catholic Worker movement. Under the watchful eye of Cardinal Mundelein, the Chicago Church was nurturing a generation of Catholic liberals. The phenomenon was not limited to Chicago but that city was certainly in the lead. As the children of the Church's immigrant groups began to grow, they assimilated the values of their parents' adopted country. But they were growing up in a time of social and economic convolution and many of these children had enough confidence, education and sophistication to want to influence systems which they felt could exert positive change. On the other hand, these children were not so far removed from their parents that they did not recognize their Church as an agent of change. These dynamics of social and economic flux, assimilation and education created the largest if not the first generation of Catholic liberals the American immigrant Church ever produced. [1]

------

[1]In his history of American Catholicism, Jay Dolan speaks of an earlier group of Cathlic liberals nurtured on the republican philosophy of the eighteenth and early nineteenth centuries, but this group had been overwhelmed by the mass migration of immigrants after 1840 and its implications. See Dolan, *The American Catholic Experience*, pp. 102-118.

Dorothy Day was close to this generation in terms of age but not spirit. Her education and experience had led her to a radical's perspective which did not include the same faith in time and process which her liberal proteges shared. Initially this very basic difference meant little. They all shared a religious faith which had in its history transcended much greater philosophic breeches and they shared a commitment to the call for social reform implicit in their Faith. But Dorothy Day's pacifism which sprang from her radicalism would eventually cause an irrevocable split in the movement. She was a socialist-turned-Catholic and she was able to weave the principles of both into a neat pattern. While a socialist she had opposed the First World War because it had set worker against worker. Later as a Catholic, she opposed the Spanish Civil War because it set one part of the "Mystical Body of Christ" against another. While most of the Catholic press and hierarchy supported Franco, Dorothy Day used her paper to begin to work out a theory of Catholic pacifism and condemend both sides in the conflict for the carnage they were inflicting on each other.[2]

She objected to those who linked the survival of Catholicism to a Franco victory. To her, the greatest threat to Christianity was not the leftist government of the Spanish republic, but rather the hate precipitated by the war itself. She noted that the Carlists supporters of Franco shouted "For Christ the King" as they went into battle and wondered if it was for "Christ the King that they killed?"

"When no one thinks any longer of fraternity or duties of charity, it is then", she wrote, "that as Catholics and among Catholics we have to condemn the wrong sense of those who deliver

---

[2]Aside from the *Catholic Worker*, only *Commonweal* and Chicago's diocesan paper, *New World* pursued a neutral course during the Spanish Civil War.

themselves up to violence, to insult and to reprisals for the sake of pagan principles."[3]

Being well grounded in the theology of conscience, Dorothy Day's liberal Catholic supporters had little trouble accepting her pacifism during the Spanish conflict. In fact, most liberal Catholics agreed with her. The war hardly affected the United States, the country remained officially neutral (despite the fact that Texaco oil fueled Franco's army, and young Americans were fighting for the Republic) and there were more immediate problems which bound Catholic liberals together. *The Chicago Catholic Worker* hardly mentioned the conflict in Spain and when the editors did, they accepted Dorothy Day's position.

The Spanish Civil War which precipitated the development of Catholic Worker pacifism, proved to be a mere flexing of muscles by those powers who wished to bring a new order to Europe. The fascists encouraged by their victories in Spain, and the democracies frightened by them both accelerated preparations for the conflict they deemed inevitable, and three months after Franco's victory the war for Europe exploded.

Americans were immediately swept into the whirl of the European embroilment, and agitation for preparedness proliferated. Echoing the warnings of Dorothy Day, Catholic Workers in Chicago took grim note of the European conflict and the call to arms precipitating in America. "In a mad scramble we rush forward with an armament program" John Cogley noted. But the huge allocations for military production would not provide security, he warned, "it would only serve as an occasion for furthering the rapidly increasing war hysteria."[4] In the months leading up to the war, the *Chicago Catholic Worker* continued to editorialize against the military preparedness campaign being waged across the country. A com-

---

[3]*Catholic Worker*, December 1936.

[4]*Chicago Catholic Worker*, June 1940.

mon theme in the Chicago paper was conscience, and to the editors it was unconscionable that the government which had been curtailing relief funds, had suddenly found billions for armaments. In the 1950's liberals would rail against those who sacrificed domestic programs for increased defense spending against the Communist threat. They argued that unless America were economically secure, threats to democracy would come from within rather than without the borders. Cogley, who as editor of *Commonweal* in the fifties was recognized as a leading liberal intellectual, had already proposed this rationale in the Chicago Catholic Worker just prior to World War II.

"Not by arms alone", he wrote, "can we defend ourselves and our values." Because "as long as there were millions of unemployed there would exist within our country a lure to the security provided by totalitarian states". He pointed out that it was a "short view of things which imagin[ed] moral preparations inferior to the piling up of weapons."[5]

In New York, Dorothy Day also stepped up the anti-war campaign . While the Chicago group approached the issue as a matter of individual conscience, Dorothy Day was moving the paper toward a position of doctrinaire pacifism. When the government announced its plans to begin military conscription, Dorothy published a series of articles by Monsignor Barry O'Toole which concluded that the draft was morally indefensible.[6]

As Dorothy intensified the Catholic Worker peace campaign, new influences began to permeate the movement. The most imposing of which was John Hugo, a staunch pacifist who had an increasingly more powerful influence on Dorothy Day. "No doubt pacifism is clear to you" he wrote to her, "but you have not tried to work it out doctrinally. Pacifism must proceed from truth",

---

[5]Ibid.

[6]*Catholic Worker*, January 1940-September 1940.

he assserted, "or it cannot exist at all."[7]
Father Hugo's criticism of Dorothy Day's early
pacifism was confirmed by the recollections of
Monsignor John Hayes who came to know her when he
acted as chaplain for the Chicago Catholic
Worker. He remembered that Dorothy had been in
his words, "an overzealous pacifist" and it was
the force of her personality not her philosophy
which had convinced many around the house to
affirm the pacifist position. Consequently,
"after Pearl Harbor, many of the young men in the
group were unprepared to defend their pacifism"
He recalled one "outspoken pacifist who became a
bayonet instructor after the war began".[8]
Although the pacifism of the Catholic Worker can
not be dismissed with one simple vignette, both
Father Hugo's and Msgr. Hayes' observations
regarding Dorothy Day's pacifism contain a degree
of truth. In 1940 no one knew this better than
Dorothy Day herself and during the war years she
struggled with the theology of pacifism. It con-
sumed her as no other issue would and in the
process transformed her and the Catholic Worker
movement.

Even before becoming a Catholic, Dorothy Day
had developed a radical anti-bourgeois view.
She had rejected nationalism as a fulfillment of
the need for community, and materialism as an
adequate substitute for the longings of the
spirit. Her friends in those days were mostly
socialists who had come to similar conclusions.
As she had rejected the end to which she perceived the bourgeois world moving, she also
rejected their means, which she observed to be
unbridled competition, exploitation, and a super
nationalism which inevitably led to war. Along
with her socialist friends, she opposed the Great
War which in a gush of patriotism and false unity
had set worker against worker. Although
socialism gave form to her criticism it did not

---

[7]Miller, *Harsh and Dreadful Love*, p.166.

[8]Hayes interview.

provide substance for her spiritual inclinations. This she found in the Catholic Church. Upon becoming a Catholic, she found spiritual sustenance in the concept of the Mystical Body of Christ, but her social conscience did not settle until she met Peter Maurin and discovered how to make spiritual abstractions a workable reality. Peter Maurin had introduced Dorothy Day to the social implications of her faith, but it was her own radicalism that took Peter Maurin's vision to its logical conclusion: Catholic pacifism.

In the 1930's the Catholic Worker had been many things to many people, and those who had journeyed with Dorothy in a spirit of certainty and righteousness in the early days of the movement now suffered with her in these days of soulful struggle. Many had come to the Worker movement because of their Catholicism, but now the movement was taking them into unexplored and questionable theological regions of their faith. Pacifism opened up dangerous and speculative concepts to those who had been basing their social thought on authority no less than papal encyclicals, and it was difficult for many to now simply follow the *Catholic Worker*'s encyclicals. Dorothy's preoccupation with pacifism distressed many readers of the *Catholic Worker*. "The pacifism you preach is false, unpatriotic and dangerous", one woman wrote, and she asked Dorothy not to spend one cent of what she sent her on "pacifist propaganda". A priest from Louisianna who had been instrumental in the labor movement and in starting a Catholic Worker house in Houma wrote to Dorothy to "urge you with all my heart to change your stand."[9]

Father H.A. Rinehold wrote to Dorothy to explain that the *Catholic Worker* was no longer read or distributed at the Seattle Worker house. "It is filled almost entirely with pacifism" which, he explained, "tended to arouse pacifists to new outbursts that were far from pacifistic".

---

[9]Miller, *Harsh and Dreadful Love*, pp.167-168.

They would continue however, he told Dorothy Day, to read the *Chicago Catholic Worker*.[10]

The Chicago Catholic Workers maintained that there was no final "Catholic" position on the war. "Until the Pope speaks" they believed that it was "the right and obligation of every Catholic to form his own conscience on the issue of war." Although the paper never advocated intervention, and they did print articles against conscription and preparedness, they never presented their position as dogma nor hinted that because one did not accept this position they were not abiding by principles of the Cathollic Church or the Worker movement. They merely presented their arguments as instruments to help in the formation of a sound conscience on the issue. The fact that one of the editors (Cogley) eventually joined the army and the other (Marciniak) became a conscientious objector underscores the evenhandedness with which the issue was addressed. Editorially, the paper urged Catholics to enlist the teachings of the Church fathers to reach their conclusions on the war. They rejected the pacifist position that all war was inherently wrong, and maintained that Catholics had a duty to ascertain the morality of the specific conflict. The position taken by the Chicago Worker had become a popular one in the thirties as Catholics, caught up in the pacifism of the decade, tried to find in their own tradition a moral valuation for war. As a result the Catholic Association for International Peace was formed as an offshoot of the National Catholic Welfare Council and a theology on modern war was developed. Written by Father Cyprian Emmanuel, it was a doctrine based on the Augustinian and Thomistic theories of a just war. The conclusion reached by Emmanuel was that in a modern war it woulds be extremely difficult to fulfill the requirements of a just war and knowing this Catholics might, in the event of another war want to consider becoming pacifists. The N.C.W.C.

[10]Ibid., p.168.

published Emmanuel's conclusions in leaflet form and distributed them on College campuses throughout the nation.[11]

This action by the N.C.W.C. was probably in part a Catholic response to the international Oxford movement which was spreading the campuses at that time. The fact that many thought the Oxford movement was Communist inspired probably motivated the Catholic hierarchy into action as much as anything. Until 1941 the just war theory as modernized by Emmanuel, served to convince most Catholics, including the Chicago Catholic Workers, that America should not involve itself in the European conflict.

According to a survey of 50,000 Catholic college students, Father Cyprian's argument convinced 18,000 of them that they ought to be conscientious objectors should America become involved in another war and eighty-three percent felt that there should be a referendum before ever sending troops into conflict. Catholic students, *Christian Century* magazine noticed, were beginning to do some critical thinking on war and that process went far "beyond the routine acceptance of the excellent slogan 'Keep America out of war'".[12]

Despite their philosophic differences, the Chicago Catholic Worker and its New York counterpart seemed united on the issue of pacifism. Although the Chicagoans usually avoided the issue in print, they did editorialize against the draft bill when it became law in 1940. They warned that conscription was a tool of totalitarian regimes and they also published in the same

---

[11]Cyprian Emmanuel, O.F.M. Ph.D., "The Morality of War," CAIP files Series 10 Box 5 (Milwaukee, Wisconsin, Marquette University Archives).

[12]N.C.W.C. News Service Release, November 14, 1939, CAIP files Series 10, Box 4, Marquette UNiversity Archives, Milwaukee, Wisconsin; "Catholic Students Are Against War," Christian Century, 56 (November 22, 1939).

inssue an explanation of the Catholic pacifist position of the New York *Catholic Worker*.

During the early years of the war in Europe the complete pacifism of the New York Catholic Worker and the just war theory based pacifism of the Chicago group had led both to conclusions that were barely distinguishable. Both had opposed preparedness and the draft law. But as the war in Europe intensified, and the atrocities of the Hitler regime became more apparent, many began to see the evil of Nazism as a justification for war. Although the number of pro-war Chicago Catholic Workers began to increase, this view was kept out of the paper. Apparently they did not want to accentuate their differences with the New York group. They did however continue to debate the issue among themselves. Cogley, and a number of others were gradually moving to the interventionist position. They argued that the conditions necessary for a just war were certainly fulfilled in the conflict against Hitler.

Using the same theories and information Ed Marciniak reached the opposite conclusion. Writing to John Cogley he confessed that although he was aware of the "horrendous menace of Nazism", he could not advocate intervention. He saw no difference between the Nazi system and the very means with which Hitler was being fought. Therefore, he concluded, "I can not give my allegience to that system and I must refuse my cooperation". The majority at the Chicago house of hospitality did not agree with Marciniak. They began to see a moral obligation to terminate the Nazi menace. The Chicagoans' point of view reflected opinions across the nation including the other Catholic Worker houses.

Dorothy Day was becoming increasingly disturbed by the drift of the Catholic Worker away from pacifism. And as her commitment to pacifism intensified, so did her conviction to bring the rest of the Catholic Worker along with her. In August 1940, she sent a letter to all the Catholic Worker houses which Tom Sullivan

later referred to as "Dorothy's encyclical". In
it she reaffirmed her pacifism and stated that
would be the Catholic Worker's position also.
"There are some members of the Catholic Worker
who do not stand with us on this issue", she
wrote. Some had even taken it upon themselves to
suppress the paper. Since there was such a close
connection between the philosophy of the Catholic
Worker and pacifism, she declared that those who
headed Catholic Worker houses across the country
ought to be pacifists.[13] This proclamation by
Dorothy Day troubled Cogley and he confessed as
much to his colleagues. He had not yet reached a
final conclusion on the war issue, but when he
did it would be an issue of conscience, not doctrinaire pacifism. He told his friends that if
this disagreement with Dorothy were not settled
soon, he would have to give up his work at the
Catholic Worker house. Others were also disturbed by Dorothy's letter. In Seattle Father
Rinehold responded, "I do not approve of this at
all. I wonder if you can take a whole movement
which stands for far more things than conscription and tag it on this one issue throwing out
all those who do not agree with you." He also
condemned her for adopting "dictator's methods,
laying down party lines and purging dis-
senters."[14]
Dorothy was not moved by this rationaliza-
tion. To her, peace was at the core of the

---

[13]O'Gara interview; Sullivan interview. William
Miller cites this letter in his history of the
Catholic Worker. He emphasizes the fact that
Dorothy was disturbed that the Seattle group had
suppressed the paper; Miller, <u>Harsh and Dreadful
Love</u>, p.168.

[14]Reinhold's conviction that Hitler must be
opposed had a strong basis. He had recently been
forced to leave his home in Germany because of
his beliefs and his activism there. See Cogley *A
Canterbury Tale*, p.37; also Miller, *Harsh and
Dreadful Love*, p.168.

Worker movement and without that the movement was
nothing more than an organization of do-gooders.
She was as zealous as any saint with a vision,
and she pursued a course which the less saintly
and more practical could not understand. Dorothy
continued to fret over the drift in the movement,
and a year after she had written her ultimatum,
she sent another letter. She announced that
there would be a retreat at the Catholic Worker
farm in Easton, Pennsylvania. "All Catholic
Workers should come", she advised, "there will be
no excuse -- we have taken a wife. . ., we have
bought a new farm. . . , we have a new yoke of
oxen. . . .,-- would not do. We must drop everything listening to the Lord who will speak only
if we keep silent."[15]

But to many it was not the Lord who spoke to
them that weekend . Dorothy had asked Father
John Hugo, the pacifist to lead the retreat, and
the priest spent the weekend indoctrinating the
participants. Cogley, O'Gara and Sullivan
returned from the Catholic Worker farm more distressed than before. It became clear to them
while they were in Pennsylvania that Dorothy was
taking the Worker into an area where they could
not follow and they would have to abandon the
movement which had played such an important part
in the last four years of their lives.[16]

On his return to Chicago, Cogley decided
that there would be no more issues of the *Chicago
Catholic Worker*. It was Dorothy's movement , she
had elicited her position, and there were more
important things to do with his life than to be
the leader of the loyal opposition to a woman he
deeply respected and loved. While many of the
Catholic Workers returned home and sought defer-
ments, Cogley had a hard time trying to enlist.

Monsignor Reynold Hillenbrand had taken it
upon himself to explain to Cogley's draft board
the significance of the young man's work on Blue

---

[15]Ibid., p.188.

[16]Cogley, *A Canterbury Tale*, p.32.

Island Avenue.   The draft board, dominated by Italian Catholics, was impressed with the letter from the well known director of the seminary and they granted Cogley a deferment.   Cogley however, could not accept the deferment for being director of the Catholic Worker house.   Not only did he believe in the justness of the war, but to accept a deferral based on his duties at the Catholic Worker would seem at least duplicitous consider- ing his recent arguments in favor of interven- tion at the Easton retreat.   He finally reached a compromise with his adament draft board.   They would induct him, but only after he had found a home for each of the men living at the Catholic Worker house.   The Little Sisters of the poor volunteered to take all of his charges and within two months of the Pennsylvania retreat, the Catholic Worker house on Blue Island Avenue was closed. With his induction imminent, Cogley married Theodora Schmidt and shortly after their honeymoon he entered the army.[17]

Soon the war was upon them, and caught up in the sweep of events the Catholic Workers had little time to reflect on the demise of their community.   Jim O'Gara had been drafted along with Tom Sullivan.   Marty Paul and John Doebble applied for Conscientious Objector status on the basis of their religious convictions and had been sent to the Catholic Conscientious Objectors camp in New Hampshire.   Ed Marciniak was granted a deferment and he immersed himself in the labor movement and earned a living by teaching part- time at Loyola University.

After a while the Catholic Worker movement returned to Chicago.   A group of Catholic con- scientious objectors at the Alexian Brothers Hospital opened a house in 1942 at 1208 Webster Street.   There would be other houses in Chicago in the decades that followed, but they told a far different story than the one shared by those who had gathered together in the 1930's.   After Dorothy Day clarified her position on the war,

---

[17]Ibid.

the character of the Worker movement changed. In the early days the movement comprised all those who had a sense of social justice: liberal reformer, moderate and radical had gathered at the same table to share energy and ideas.

For the most part, the Chicago Workers had supported the movement because Catholic Worker ideas approximated their own. Their views however were based in their religious commitment, and their religious convictions were grounded in a tradition which included respect for family and other institutions which had nurtured their faith. They did not advocate a radical departure from their roots, only an alteration of direction. Although they remained committed to social reform, it had to take place within forms which respected their philosophic foundation. A faith that in time, these insitutions could progress in the direction of humanity remained at the root of their thought.

Dorothy Day had no such faith in bourgeois concepts of progress. As a result of Maurin's indoctrination, she had embraced a radical eschatological view which contradicted the mythology of progress in time. Dorothy Day was thoroughly Catholic, but her perspective differed greatly from her counterparts at the Chicago Catholic Worker. She was a convert to the Faith and therefore her intellectual and spiritual commitment was unfettered by conventions that were intertwined with the Catholicism of those born in the Faith. Furthermore, even before becoming a Catholic, she had gone through a purging iconoclasm as a socialist. Therefore when she developed a religious commitment it led her to a radical Christianity which did not tolerate the institutions and conventions her more liberal counterparts felt necessary. She had a complete love and respect for liturgy, churches and saints, but only in so far as they clarified the duties and obligations that one person had for another. She was hardly tolerant of bishops who sat with bankers or priests who advocated intervention into a bourgeois, nationalist war.

Although the dream of most liberal Catholics was to Christianize American life, there was little that she saw worthy of incorporation into true Christianity. When she saw the name Rockefeller, for example, she did not think of foundations, but rather of heads being smashed on a picket line. If her radicalism seemed threatening so be it. She believed Christianity should be a menace not a solace to all time-serving institutions.

For Dorothy Day, the Catholic Worker provided a counterpoint to American idealism. The significance of the Catholic Worker was that it outlined Christianity as a cooperative, peaceful vision of community. It did not make a virtue of "fair-play","opportunity" and "competition". Its idea of progress moved toward an infinite vision not a finite goal. It was through focusing on the infinite, on Christ's promise of community, that humans would find peace and true solidarity. If any idea is to be believable it must be liveable, and therefore Dorothy Day set out to live an uncompromising Christianity. She followed the words of St. Teresa who said "All the way to heaven is heaven." Her life became the embodiment of an idea whose central message was peace. In this role she demonstrated the fortitude and intransigence of a saint. Saints are difficult to emulate, but they are rare gifts in this weary, time-bound world and they provide a sweet glimpse of the possibilities of life and eternity.

The Chicago Workers for the most part shared Dorothy's commitment, but not her radicalism. Even Ed Marciniak, who remained in Chicago as a conscientious objector, felt that the greatest contribution of the Catholic Worker in Chicago was not its radical vision but rather the practical accomplishments it had achieved.Through the Catholic Worker thousands of hungry men had been fed, blacks had found another voice raised in their defense, as had Jews, and through the *Chicago Catholic Worker*, unions had a publication which presented labor's side in their struggle with capitalists. Now all that was gone.

In New York an air of melancholy had
engulfed the Worker house. The vibrant
enthusiasm of the thirties was gone. Peter
Maurin who had remained silent on the issue of
pacifism, had suddenly grown old and lost his
spark.[18] The long lines that had characterized
the Worker house were now forming at recruiting
stations , and word came in almost daily of
Ctholic Worker houses across the country closing
down. The Catholic Worker was suffering the dif-
fusive and painful force of the war and Dorothy
Day pondered its fate as many began to speak of
the movement in the past tense.

Before going to their assigned camps, Tom
Sullivan and John Cogley visited Dorothy Day in
New York. She was glad to see them and as members of the family she welcomed them. She did,
however try to persuade them one last time. To
her arguments, Sullivan responded, "Hitler won't
be persuaded by pietistic phrases, Dorothy; the
only thing he understands is a gun put to his
head."[19]

Not only a majority of the Catholic Workers
but even her old radical friends failed to

---

[18]Miller, *Harsh and Dreadful Love,* p.174. After
the war, Tom Sullivan lived at and managed the
Catholic Worker house in New York. During this
time he personally cared for Maurin until his
death in 1949. It is Sullivan's belief that
Maurin viewed the war as a necessary evil to rid
the world of the Nazi terror. He felt this way
especially after June, 1940 when Germany overran
France, his homeland. Although Maurin wrote
little on the subject, Sullivan believed that his
views regarding international relations leaned
toward the idea of a strong United Nations. But
it would have to be God centered. His biographer
points out that Maurin believed, as he did with
other issues, "that intelligent people are turning to the Church as the one moral security left
in the world". Sullivan interview; Ellis, *Peter
Maurin,* p.150.

[19]Sullivan interview.

understand her pacifism. Mike Gold wrote in the
Daily Worker, "I just can't believe the mystic
who says he 'loves his enemy'." To Gold it was
the "most difficult tenet in Christian theology."
Referring to his "old friend Dorothy Day" and her
"earnest little paper", he recalled that she had
always been an honest person but he would respect
her pacifism more had she been a pacifist during
the Spanish Civil War. Implying that she had
supported Franco, he concluded that Dorothy had
been more affected by the politics of the fascists in the Catholic Church than she realized.[20]
Dorthy Day had never supported the fascists in
the Spansish Civil War (it was during that war
that her pacifism had begun to develop).
Although his conclusion was wrong, Gold's [prmise
was correct. Pacifism is one of the "most difficult of all tenets of Christian theology." But
Dorothy Day remained true to it throughout the
war and for the rest of her life.

In September 1943, Dorothy Day took a leave
of absence from the Catholic Worker. While on
retreat she could not help but think of the young
people who had strengthened the Worker movement
throughout the thirties. They were all gone now.
In the December 1943, issue of the *Catholic
Worker*, she mentioned Jim O'Gara and Tom Sullivan
on the Gilbert Islands. This was one of the
reasons she had withdrawn from the work, she
wrote, "to have time to gather and hold in my
prayers all those members of our family, all
those dear to us."

The Chicago Catholic Workers she thought
about were gone, scattered throughout the Pacific
and the United States, in army camps and conscientious objector compounds. John Bowers who
had been too old for the draft, maintained the
Catholic Worker house on Taylor Street, but the
heart of the movement, the house on Blue Island
Avenue which fed the hungry, sheltered the homeless and published a paper was gone forever.

---

[20]Miller, *Harsh and Dreadful Love*, p.172.

CHAPTER IX

ALTERNATIVES TO WAR

In the winter of 1944, Dorothy Day received a letter from Tom Sullivan on the Gilbert Islands in the Pacific. "I often think of you", he wrote. "My thoughts go back to you at odd times such as torrid days while perspiring in a plane, lying on a cot at night staring at the toip of my tent. . . skipping mud puddles to and from work and so on."[1] After the war when he returned to the Catholic Worker, Sullivan often reminded those who had followed Dorothy Day's pacifism that he an others like him had suffered a great deal "to protect you lousy C.O.'s."[2] But Sullivan had chosen to fight in the war as a matter of conscience and likewise, the pacifists had made an equally difficult decision based on their convictions.

The decision to be a conscientious objector was especially difficult for Catholics. Within a Church which prided itself on its contributions in time of war, these Catholic C.O.'s found themselves abandoned in a sea of suspicion and contempt. One priest who was a member of a draft board told a Catholic seeking C.O. status, " I am a priest and they are sending them right along. . . if you have been reading scripture to reach this conclusion you must be misinterpreting them"[3] Although as late as October 31, 1941, *Commonweal* magazine reported that 91.5 % of

---

[1]Miller, *Harsh and Dreadful Love*, p.194.

[2]Dwight Mc Donald, "The Foolish Things of the World," *New Yorker* (October 4, 1952): p.58.

[3]Gordon Zahn, "A Study of the Social Backgrounds of Catholic Conscientious Objectors in Civilian Public Service During World War II," (M.A. thesis, Catholic University of America, 1950), p.6.

Catholic priests interviewed opposed American
entry into a shooting war outside the Western
Hemisphere, Catholic leaders quickly reversed
themselves once the reality of war was upon
them.[4] Thomas Maynard, writing for *American Mercury*, took note of the *Commonweal* article and
predicted correctly, "Of one thing we can be perfectly sure: the moment America gets into the war
openly nobody will be more vociferously patriotic
than Catholics".[5] Fulfilling this prophecy when
the war broke out, The Catholic bishops issued a
joint statement which affirmed that "America was
fighting a righteous war" and urged "all
Catholics to unite in praying for victory. . ."[6]
    To those Catholics who thought that partici-
pation in the war might be a matter of personal
conscience, the Jesuit writer Wilfred Parsons
advised that "it is beyond the competency of the
individual to arrive at any judgement on this
matter. . . ." The government, he asserted has
the right to direct "the external actions of the
citizens to the common good of the community."
He concluded that it should be obvious that there
is "nothing in the teaching of the Catholic
Church which states that the citizen is exempt
from the obligation of bearing arms in a war. . .
regardless of whether it is just or unjust."[7]
    One Catholic C.O. writing from a camp,
stated that unlike the Mennonites, Quakers or
members of other "peace churches", Catholics at
the alternative service camp did not enjoy the

---

[4]"Clergy Poll," *Commonweal* 35 (October 31,
1941): p.37.

[5]Thomas Maynard, "Catholics and Nazis,"
American Mercury 53 (October, 1941): pp.391-400.

[6]"Stand on War", *Time* 40 (November 23,
1942.:p.24.

[7]Wilfred Parsons, "Can a Catholic Be a Conscientious Objector?" *Commonweal* 34 (June 27,
1941): p.226.

support of "a tradition we must uphold. . . . Our place in C.P.S. [Civilian Public Service]", he wrote, "is more personal, more individual. . ."[8] Ed Marciniak, writing to his friend John Cogley who had enlisted in the army, described his own pacifism as a"seeming handicap which I possess in communicating with my fellow brothers in Christ."[9]

In order to overcome this sense of alienation that Catholic pacifists suffered within their own Church, the Catholic Worker in 1941 took it upon themselves to organize an unprecedented movement in American Catholicism: The Association of Catholic Conscientious Objectors (A.C.C.O.).[10] This group eventually became aligned with the National Service Board of Religious Objectors (N.S.B.R.O.) and became one of the four original sponsers of the Alternative Service Camps established during World War II. The N.S.B.R.O., comprised of members of the traditional peace churches, had been formed shortly after the Selective Service Act passed in 1940. It was the desire of the N.S.B.R.O. to establish a series of conscientious objector

---

[8]*Catholic C.O.*, January, 1944. This paper which was published quarterly (with a few exceptions) from September 1943 until September, 1945 contained articles reflecting the views of many Catholic pacifists. Gordon Zahn, a sociologist, who was also a Catholic C.O., co-edited this paper and remarked years later that he was "impressed that this official quarterly did catch the prevailing temper and attitudes and opinions expressed in the camps as he remembers them". Gordon Zahn, *War Conscience and Dissent*, (New York: Hawthorn Books, 1967), p.172.

[9]Marciniak to Cogley, August 30, 1943. Marciniak papers.

[10]Zahn, *War, Conscience and Dissent*, p. 163; also interview with Arthur Sheehan, New York City, August 9, 1972.

camps throughout the country which would run independently from the Selective Service.[11] Quaker leader Rufus Jones reasoned that "The great majority of the people do not believe our stand is right. Therefore we ought not let our convictions be a financial burden on them."[12]

The members of the traditional peace churches were anxious to use alternative service camps to dramatize the intrinsic idealism of the pacifist. They wanted to design work that woud exemplify their belief that people could live and work together in peace. They hoped this pattern of life would demonstrate that nations could also live together in harmony.[13] The government quickly stifled such idealism however, and the N.S.B.R.O. quickly became nothing more than an agency of the Selective Service.[14]

In February of 1941, Arthur Sheehan, director of the A.C.C.O. went to Washington to present his case for Catholic C.O.'s before the N.S.B.R.O. He explained to Paul French, head of the board, that the Catholic C.O.'s would like to have a camp set aside for members of their faith.[15] Sheehan told French that the New York

---

[11]Charles Chatfield, *For Peace and Justice: Pacifism in America* (Knoxville: The University of Tennesee Press, 1969), pp. 306-307; Lawrence Wittner, *Rebels Against War, The American Peace Movement 1941-1960*, (New York:Columbia University Press, 1969(p.71.

[12]R.E.S. Thompson, "Onward Christian Soldiers," *Saturday Evening Post*, August 16, 1941, p.53.

[13]Chatfield, *Peace and Justice*, pp.306-307; Wittner, *Rebels*, p.71.

[14]Sheehan interview; *Catholic Worker*, March 1941.

[15]Sheehan interview; *Catholic Worker,* March 1941.

Catholic Worker group owned a farm in Easton Pennsylvania which could be used by the Catholic C.O.'s. [16] The farm, Sheehan added, could operate at no expense to the government. In essence, what Sheehan had suggested was what the N.S.B.R.O. had requested the preceding year, a camp which would run independently of the Selective Service system. Although he personally approved of the plan, French explained to Sheehan that his proposal would not comply with Selective Service guidelines. he did suggest however that the government might be willing to turn over an old C.C.C. camp which the Association might transform into a Catholic alternative service camp. [17]

On April 15, 1941, Paul French sent Sheehan a telegram stating that the Selective Service had approved the request for a camp, and assigned them to an abandoned CCC center in Stoddard, New Hampshire.

The Catholics who entered the camp in June 1941 did so enthusiastically. They were determined , one wrote to Dorothy Day, "to practice the art of peace," by living and working together in harmony. [18] Despite their optimism the experiment proved a dismal failure. The insignificance of the work, coupled with the Siberian-like environment of the New England camp, caused a rapid deterioration of the men's sense of purpose. "We have our troubles here," one memebr confided, "But consider our circumstances: forty-five men forced together in a

---

[16]Sheehan interview; Miller, *Harsh and Dreadful Love,* pp.165-166.

[17]Sheehan interview. A number of Civilian Conservation Corps Camps had been used for this purpose. These were camps which had been established during the early days of the Roosevelt administrtion to give young men an opportunity to work.

[18]*Catholic Worker,*November 1941.

crowded place, doing what we think is unimportant work and living in what for the most part are crude quarters at very cold temperatures, thus we have our irritations our weariness"[19]

The camp eventually closed when the financial pressures became overwhelming. Unlike other pacifists, the Catholics received no support from their Church. Some of the peace churches attempted to help the A.C.C.O., but the costs of their own C.O. programs limited their generosity.[20] The also received small donations from groups such as the Fellowship of Reconciliation, the American Civil Liberties Union as well as from various Catholic Worker houses still in existence.[21] The contributions never exceeded the deficits however, and the camp was forced to close in March, 1943. Despite the fact that Congress had set funds aside to compensate and maintain C.O.'s in alternative service camps, the Selective Service spent none of the money. For six years C.O.'s put in over eight million man days of free work in the United States at no cost to the government, but at a cost to the peace groups of seven million dollars. The brunt of this bill was born by the historic peace churches. But for the Catholic C.O.'s, without the support of their coreligionists the cost became a

---

[19]*Catholic Worker,*July-August 1942.

[20]For example in January, 1943 the *Catholic Worker* reported, "Eighty-five percent of the Mormon C.P.S. camp observed the second anniversary of the first draft registration by fasting. The amount saved, $13.44, was donated to the Catholic Worker."

[21]*Catholic Worker* March 1941.

personal one.[22]

    Although the New England project ended in failure, a successful Catholic Conscientious Objector program was launched in Chicago at the Alexian Brothers Hospital. In March, 1942 after many persuasive letters and personal appeals the Selective Service permitted a group of Catholics under the leadership of John Doebble to organize a camp at the Chicago hospital on Belden Avenue. This was the first such project allowed and its success caused hospital work to become a common form of alternative service in the later years of the war.[23] Officials had hoped to keep the conscientious objectors in rural areas isolated from public contact, since they did not want the views of the C.O.'s to receive any attention which might disrupt the efficiency of the war propaganda apparatus on the homefront. It was only after a concentrated and persuasive effort by understaffed hospitals, the A.C.L.U. and the various peace organizations that the government,

---

[22]Wittner, *Rebels*, p.72; Walter Roe, "Conscientious Objectors," *New Republic* (January 8, 1945): p.49. The difficulties of the Catholic C.O.'s is revealed in a letter published in the March 1942 issue of the *Catholic Worker:* "Many of the C.O.'s are not able to pay the $35 a month needed as their share of the expenses. . . the men who are drafted and who are given the status of C.O.'s are forced to pay for themselves, or be supported by the Association [A.C.C.O.] which of course has no assets at all being made up of C.O.'s themselves".

[23]Mulford Sibley and Phillip E. Jacob, *Conscription of Conscience, The American State and the Conscientious Objector 1940-1947*, (Ithaca: Cornell University Press, 1952), p.190.

specifically the Selective Service, relented.[24]

Doebble, a former associate of the Chicago Catholic Worker, was encamped in New England at the time, and he readily accepted the responsibility for the Chicago project.[25] Not only did the new camp allow him to escape the barren wilderness of New England, but it also provided an opportunity to perform significant alternative service. Working and living in an urban environment also made life more bearable for the conscientious objectors. Most of them had come from cities, and the isolated life in a forestry camp had contributed greatly to their disillusionment with the project. The city with its myriad entertainments, libraries and colleges promised to make their confinement less burdensome.[26]

Most of the men at the Alexian Brothers Hospital camp had become conscientious objectors due to their asociation with the Catholic Worker movement. In order to demonstrate their continued commitment to the Catholic Worker they established a house of hospitality. "St. Joseph's house of hospitality has a new address", Jim Rogan announced in the *Catholic Worker*, "1208 Webster, just one block away from the Alexian

---

[24]As Walter Roe pointed out, "Expediency has dominated the government's policy of isolating objectors in remote outposts". See: "Conscientious Objectors", *New Republic* (January 8, 1945): p.49.

[25]Interview, John Doebble, Chicago, Illinois, May 15, 1976; *Catholic Worker*, March 1942.

[26]*Catholic Worker*, May 1944. Psychiatrist Anton Boisen stated, "One factor in the better morale of the hospital units as contrasted with the camps is to be found in the sense of independence on the part of the hospital workers." See: "C.O.'s Their Morale in Church Operated Service," *Psychiatry* 7 (May, 1967): p.22.

hospital" They began the new venture in "fear and trembling" he continued, "because we know the great good that was done at Blue Island Avenue".[27]

It probably comforted Dorothy Day to know that there was a new Catholic Worker house in Chicago. Although they might not equal "the great good that was done at Blue Island Avenue", during those times of trial, the mere existence of a Catholic Worker house marked a significant accomplishment. The vitality of youth on which the Catholic Worker had thrived in the thirties was now being sapped by another crusade. The movement had also lost many followers because of its pacifist stand. One priest wrote to Dorothy Day, "A rather unfortunate thing happened in my church this morning that makes it advisable for me to ask you to discontinue sending the *Catholic Worker*". The pastore explained that his assistant objected to the *Catholic Worker*'s position on pacifism, which he said was "against the teaching of moral theologians and against . . . the Bishops of the country who sent word to our President telling him they were in utter cooperation with him in the present crisis." The priest feared that if he continued to distribute the paper it would appear that he was acting "against episcopal authority."[28]

The scene at this particular pastor's church was reinacted throughout the country as subscriptions to the *Catholic Worker* decreased by over

---

[27]*Catholic Worker* July-August 1942. Before the war Rogan ran a Catholic Worker house in Baltimore, Maryland.

[28]Reverend George Smith to Catholic Worker, March 10, 1942. Catholic Worker Papers (Milwaukee Wisconsin: Marquette University Archives).

100,000 during the war years.[29] In addition the number of Catholic Worker houses fell from over thirty-five in 1939, to eight in 1942.[30] "Although we have no immediate plans", Jim Rogan explained, at least there was another house of hospitality in Chicago where "we can shelter and feed some of the . . .poor who have no refuge."[31] Eventually they held discussion sessions which featured guest speakers. The first person to address the group was James Farmer who was, at that time, interracial secretary for the Fellowship of Reconciliation. Ed Marciniak visited the new Worker house and gave lectures there frequently. They also began a study program which was geared , they hoped, toward rebuilding a world torn by war. In this study program they learned foreign languages and customs and anything that might help them contribute to post war reconstruction in Europe.[32]

Another project which made alternative service more bearable was the opportunity to attend nursing school there. This program became especially attractive when the men learned that hours spent in the classroom would count as work hours. Eleven men graduated form the nursing program, and others graduated from special classes in pharmacology, oxygen therapy, and anesthesiology.

---

[29]In May 1939, subscriptions numbered 190,000; in January 1942 they stood at 75,000. See: Nancy Roberts, *Dorothy Day and the Catholic Worker*, (Albany: State University of New York Press, 1984), p. 180.

[30]*Catholic Worker,*January, 1943.

[31]Ibid., July-August 1942.

[32]The hope of contributing to post war reconstruction was a high priority among all C.O.'s and after the war they were instrumental in developing the C.A.R.E. program which was directed by the former director of the Conscientious Objectors, Paul French.

There were other outlets for the men's creative impulses also, as one group assembled a small publication based on the work being done at the hospital entitled *Of Human Importance*.

From the letters that Dorothy Day received, it appeared that the C.O.'s at the Alexian Brothers Hospital found their experience at the Chicago camp far more appropriate and bearable than the one in New England. The hospital work allowed them a great deal more independence, and the staff there, although they did not agree with the position the men had taken on the war, at least appreciated the extra help they provided. One of the conscientious objectors called relations with the staff "perfect". While they "don't agree with our principles", he wrote,"at least they do not discriminate against us, and we find the administration most kind and generous in caring for our needs."[33]

In spite of the good relations with the hospital and the favorable ambience the camp provided, some discontent still remained. In June, 1943, John Doebble reported that four men had left the hospital camp. He explained in the *Catholic Worker*, that the men had resigned in order to emphasize their oppositio to conscription, which they had come to perceive as involuntary servitude.

Eventually those who deserted camp ended up in prison. These men felt that they were carrying their pacifism to its logical conclusion. Not only did they refuse to take part in the killing, but they refused to comply with Selective Service. These men had taken the extremist position that any cooperation at all with the government and any action less than active resistance was contributing to the war effort. They found support for their position from Dorothy Day. Although she lent assistance, both spiritual and material, to Catholics in C.O. camps, she herself opposed the system. "If women

---

[33]Sibley and Jacob, *Conscription*, pp.190-193; *Catholic Worker*, February 1944.

become eligible for the draft", she editorialized, (there had been some discussion of this in
1943) I shall not register because I believe
modern warfare to be murder, imcompatible with a
religion of love." The only way to do away with
war , she declared, "was to do away with conscription."[34]

During the Second World War, many conscientious objectors agreed with Dorothy Day's
assesment of Selective Service. Over one-third
of the C.O.'s in the country chose prison over
compliance with the system.[35] Incarceration
proved even more unbearable than life in the most
desolate alternative service camp. Imprisoned
pacifists spent most of their time in solitary
confinement and when not there they were shunned,
ridiculed and sometimes even attacked by other
inmates who may have had character flaws but were
none the less patriotic.[36]

One superintendant of a large prison told a
C.O. entrusted to his care, "You C.O.'s may be
glad when the war is over, but not half as much
as I who yearn for the good old days of simple
murderers and bank robbers."[37] Despite the fact
that they caused and received a great deal of
trouble in prison, the Selective Service made
energetic attempts to persuade parole boards to
keep C.O.'s behind bars.[38] Walter Roe reported
that there were eight times as many C.O.'s in
prison during World War II than during the First
World War. This occured, he pointed out, in spite
of a "considerably more liberal system and with

---

[34]*Catholic Worker*, January 1943.

[35]"C.O.'s in Prison," *Christian Century* 61
(March 8, 1944): pp.302-304.

[36]Wittner, *Rebels*, p.84-85.

[37]"C.O.'s in Prison," p.303.

[38]Ibid.; see also: Wittner, *Rebels*, pp.90-
92.

officials evidently anxious to avoid issues that aroused such extensive criticism in World War I." He concluded that "the problems confronting objectors have been poorly resolved". It was obvious that policies in Washington could not control the emotions and politics of local draft boards.

It was a hard time to be a conscientious objector. Unlike World War I, few liberals and intellectuals were or became disillusioned with the causes and results of the Second World War. Due to the nature of the enemy, the righteousness of the cause was never questioned. As one pacifist admitted "Unlike the Central Powers of World War I, The Axis nations of World War II certainly did their best to provide. . . all the normal conditions of the just war."[39] Writing about the war years later John Cogley pointed out that "those who fought it do not, a decade and a half after it was brought to a close, feel they acted irrationally." He observed that no one felt they were supporting one ideology over another, but rather those who took part in the war felt they were "defenders of national integrity, property and human life, resisting by force those who were on a rampage of destruction."[40]

World War I may have been a popular war, but World War II was deemed a necessary one. On their way to a world war for the second time, Americans did not go armed with songs, fanfare and idealism, but rather with a grim determination to end the madness raging in Europe. Since 1919 the national mood had transformed from naivete to cynicism. But as one historian has pointed out, "The average American soldier may have resented his General who lived more com-

---

[39]Wittner, *Rebels*, p.121.

[40]John Cogley, "A World Without War," in William Clancy, ed., *The Moral Dilemma of Nuclear Weapons*(New York: Church Peace Union, 1961), pp.26-27.

fortably with clean clothes and plenty of cock-
tails even more than the enemy he confronted,
[but] he nevertheless fought admirably." And
although American soldiers knew that every weapon
they had was far inferior to the German's, they
hid their anger in cynicism and fought anyway
knowing the only way out of a fighting company
was injury, death or complete mental breakdown.[41]
Those on the home front may have wondred who was
getting rich from the present war, but they met
the sacrifices demanded by total war with little
protest.

For an entire generation the issue of war
and peace became judged within the Nazi context,
and pacifism became for them an indefensible
position. Especially during the war years those
who refused to fight were thought to be as
demented as the Nazi leaders themselves. Writing
about his experience in a C.O. camp, Gordon Zahn
stated that a Baltimore psychiatrist found most
of the men at one Catholic camp "unstable: they
themselves a minority within a minority group
with no outside contacts looking forward to
nothing in their situation to sustain their
morale." Zahn recalled that once the C.O.'s
learned that the administrtion was predisposed
toward this professional opinion they used it as
a method for "going out the open door". Some of
the men who "suffered sudden depressions of
serious dimensions made it no secret to others in
the group that they were putting on an act"[42]
From 1941 to 1945 any man of draft age not in
uniform was held in suspicion if not downright
contempt.

Without the camraderie of an alternative
service camp or even prison, Ed Marciniak lived

---

[41]Frederick Lewis Allen, *The Big Change
1900-1950*, (New York: Bantam Books, 1965),
pp.143-145; Paul Fussell, "The Real War 1939-
1945: An Experience in Horror and Madness,"
Atlantic 264 (August, 1989): pp. 32-48.

[42]Zahn, *Conscience and Dissent*, p. 165; also
Wittner, *Rebels*, p.92.

in Chicago during the war years as a conscientious objector. These years, which he lived
with the support of few, may have been the har-
dest of his life. Writing to his friend Cogley,
he confessed "it isn't easy, I assure you John,
to sit at home while the rest of the people you
know and love are in the thick of battle,
shouldering a gun or riding a plane. Physical
isolation is bad enough", he admitted, "but to be
isolated from the spiritual mind and mandate of
the community in which you live is a thousand
times worse". [43]

At one point he even considered joining the
medical corps and going overseas as a conscientious objector. But he changed his mind,
deciding that would be a cowardly way of avoiding
the dictates of conscience. On withdrawing this
request from the draft board he told them that
service in the medical corps would be "foolish
and insincere in my part, since even medical
service under military direction would aid toward
the continuation of the war."[44] Unable to comply
with Selective Service in any form Marciniak
implemented his own plan for waging peace.

---

[43]Marciniak to Cogley, August 30, 1943, Marciniak Papers.

[44]Marciniak's written statement to the draft
board, Marciniak Papers.

CHAPTER X

WORK

Not content to merely avoid war, Ed Marciniak hoped to actively pursue the peace for which many of his friends were fighting. He had told his draft board that he realized the "serious responsibilities [he had] shouldered as a conscientious objector", and he promised to "try with all my capabilities that God gave me to make positive contributions towards the welfare of society."[1] The basis for this new commitment he drew from lessons he had learned from his Catholic activism in the thirties.

Dorothy Day may have been correct in emphasizing the spiritual dimensions of the Catholic Worker movement, but Marciniak felt that the greatest contribution the movement had made in Chicago was the practical accomplishments of sheltering the homeless, organizing unions and raising the social consciousness of Catholics in Chicago. In order to revive the positive force which the Catholic Worker had contributed to the city, Marciniak planned a new movement and a new publication. Throughout the winter of 1942 and Spring of 1943, Marciniak laid plans for his new movement. He called his new movement the Catholic Labor Alliance (CLA) and its publication, *Work*. [2] He began this project with the same lack of funds as when he helped begin the Catholic Worker. But this time his experience and reputation made gathering funds less of a chore. he appealed by leter to many priests in the diocese who had been

------

[1]Marciniak's written statement to draft-board, Marciniak papers.

[2]Thomas Gavagan, "Five Years of *Work*", August 1948, Box 3, CCWL File, Chicago Historical Society Archives. CCWL (Chicago Council of Working Life) was a later name for the Catholic Labor Alliance.

143

LIBRARY ST. MARY'S COLLEGE

familiar with his work, and he utilized the long mailing list of the defunct *Chicago Catholic Worker*. During the year of planning, Marciniak and his friends collected over three thousand dollars with which to begin their project. In an office at the corner of State Street and Chicago Avenue which had been donated by Father Joseph Morrison, pastor of Holy Name Cathedral, Marciniak prepared the first edition of *Work*.[3]

In July, 1943, five years to the month after the first publication of the *Chicago Catholic Worker*, Marciniak completed his first issue of *Work*.[4] In it he outlined the new publication's purpose and objectives. Although it was a labor paper, he wrote that it would not be "limited to industrial relations, but rather will include all who work." *Work*, he announced will be interested in "the plight of the sharecroppers. . , racism. . , and public housing, among other things."[5] In its first year of publication, *Work* covered issues that had become quite familiar to readers of the *Chicago Catholic Worker*.

Marciniak carried a bundle of his first edition to a large factory and along with a few volunteers from the seminary, he began to distribute his new paper. As they left the factory, laborers greeted the paper with mixed reactions. "Work!" exclaimed one, "I've had enough of that all day!" Another, looking askance at the young men, commented, "Another Communist rag."[6] Others took the copies eagerly, but many more

---

[3]Ibid.

[4]Raymond John Moly, "The CLA Laboratory Test of Catholic Social Action," (M.A. Thesis, University of Notre Dame, 1950), pp. 12-13.

[5]*Work*, July 1943. Issues of this paper are on microfilm at the Chicago Historical Society.

[6]Moly "The CLA," p.14; personal interview with Ed Marciniak, Chicago Illinois, October 31, 1976.

remained skeptical.   One man wrote a letter to
Marciniak and asked, "Where were you when things
were tough? It's all right to jump on the bandwagon now," he remarked, "but we'd think more of
you if you had been around during the critical
years when the C.I.O. was organizing the steel
workers and the meatpackers."

"In 1938 when the big drive was on", Marciniak replied, "I was riding in a police patrol
wagon. Along with a few others, I was picked up
for distributing union literature for the Packinghouse Workers Organizing Committee outside the
stockyard entrance.   If that was a bandwagon", he
answered critics, "then I was on it".[7]

Actually the bandwagon he had been on in the
late thirties had the name "Catholic Worker" and
when he started this new movement he proved that
although the war had injured that movement , it
could not stifle the idealism which had created
it.   Those who read *Work* discovered the same
theology which had dominated the *Chicago Catholic
Worker*. "We believe", Marciniak wrote in his new
publication, "that a return to religion embracing
a definite program of action is the basic factor
in the solution of social problems."[8]   In addition to the newspaper, The Catholic Labor
Alliance instituted a number of labor schools.
Classes were held at the Sheil School of Social
Studies. Bishop Sheil's school which was opened
in 1943 functioned as an adult education center
in a downtown C.Y.O. (Catholic Youth Organization) building. Classes offered at the Sheil
school were the standard courses of any adult
education program, but with the influence of the
Catholic Labor Alliance, the courses which
attracted the most attention were those on the
social teachings of the Church and labor organizing.   The CLA eventually took over the Sheil
School of Social Studies and renamed it the
"Adult Education Center". But because of the

---

[7]Moly, "The CLA," p.51.

[8]*Work,* July 1943.

course curriculum and its reputation for heated discussions, the school was popularly known as "The Worker's College" or "Bishop Sheil's Labor School".[9] These classes were well attended and they fulfilled an important function, since after the demise of the Catholic Worker Movement, outside of the Communists there were very few organizations offering labor classes. Like the Communists, the CLA also used their classroom for propaganda. They indoctrinated workers on issues regarding racial and social justice, and these schools became the intellectual stimulus for a wave of Catholic social action in the 1940s and fifties.

Due to the publicity generated by the classes and the newspaper, the offices of *Work* became a community organizing center. In a pamphlet describing the day to day occurences around the offices of *Work*, Bob Sensor included the following:

> A high school student calls, "In class everybody put down unions. Is there something positive I could say?" The next day dozens of pamphlets will be sent to her.
>
> A union member kicked out of a union for committing a crime wants help to appeal to the International for readmission.
>
> A local parish wants someone to address their Holy Name Society, an Alliance member will go and give a talk on the Church and labor.[10]

---

[9]Kantowicz, *Corporation Sole*, pp.191-192; "Adult Education Center," Fall, 1944. (CCWL Files, Box 1); Andrew Greely, *The Catholic Experience* New York: Doubleday, 1969), p. 262.

[10]CCWL Files, Box 1.

Many people were responsible for the Catholic Labor Alliance, but the paper *Work* remained the brainchild of Marciniak. In a study entitled "Five Years of Work", Thomas Gavagan wrote that "Marciniak sets the policy for *Work*, he alone is responsible for it. Although he receives suggestions from members of the Alliance, they are usually concerned with matters of emphasis and coverage rather than policy."[11]

Since the worker remained "unprotected [with] little or no access to press or radio," Marciniak wanted the paper to remain primarily a labor paper. "We plan", he wrote, "to reach the rank and file worker and bring the rights of workers to those whom a union paper, even if one existed, would not reach."[12] The publication of the labor paper and its distribution outside factories throughout the Chicago area helped tremendously in labor organizing drives in the city. The president of the Chicago Federation of Labor confirmed that *Work* had been "instrumental in pointing out the good points of labor [unions] to workers who would otherwise remained uninformed".[13]

In addition to becoming an advocate of the worker, Marciniak, as he had done in the *Chicago Catholic Worker* used his new periodical to educate readers above prejudices nurtured by ignorance. Every publication of the paper contained articles dealing with racism, anti-Semitism and other issues of social injustice to which uneducated workers frequently contributed. Because of its editorial emphasis, *Work* was read by, and became a forum for Catholic priests as well as others involved in the rapidly developing social consciousness of the Chicago Catholic

---

[11]Gavagan, "Five Years of Work," p. 15.

[12]*Work*, July 1943.

[13]Gavagan, "Five Years of Work," p.15.

Church. Despite the local flavor of many of its stories, Chicago was becoming such an arresting model of Catholic social action across the nation, that the paper grew into a national publication with a circulation of over 15,000.

As he had while a member of the Catholic Worker, Marciniak took a strong stand against racism in Chicago. In *Work*, he condemned the Park Manor Investment Association and led the fight against its "united effort to keep Negroes out of the community." Marciniak's influence in Chicago grew in the forties and as it did he tried to temper the city with his idealism. Long before it became a legal matter, he told fellow citizens that it was a "moral question whether there may be any general policy in a community to keep people from getting homes simply because of their race".[14]

In order to educate fellow Catholics and to enlist the influence of the Church on the side of racial justice, Marciniak worked for the organization of the Catholic Interracial Council [CIC] in Chicago. This dream, which had begun with the interracial meetings sponsored by the Catholic Worker in the thirties, became a reality in 1944 when a Catholic Interrcial Council was finally formed. This council held forums and provided speakers in order to help fight racism in the city. In addition, they annually awarded fifty scholarships to black students so they might attend Catholic schools. In the mid fifties, Sargent Shriver was president of this group and Marciniak was a close associate. In the late fifties this council moved from the strategy of education to direct confrontation. According to William Osborne, in 1961 the CIC "was the key factor in the peaceful integration of a Negro family into suburban Skokie." The Council also lobbied for fair housing legislation, participated in the wade-in at Rainbow Beach, resolved a difficult block-busting operation on the west

---

[14]*Work*, August 1944; *Chicago Sun*, August 14, 1944.

side of the city, and testified at a public
hearing of the Temporary Woodlawn Organization in
opposition to double shift schools and for the
racial integration of schools.[15]
    Marciniak, who in the late thirties had been
chairman of the Committee of Catholics Opposed to
Anti-Semitism carried this fight into the
forties. In one issue of his paper he warned his
readers against a new group in Chicago calling
itself, the "Gentile Cooperative Association"
which was actually "an anti-Jewish organization
under a pro-Gentile cloak." He advised Catholics
especially, to keep away from this group since it
planned on "making a big play for Catholic support". He pointed out that this brand of anti-
Semitism was more dangerous than other more
blatant forms, "since their clever pro-Gentile
cover may ensnare uninformed and unsuspecting
citizens."[16] In another issue of *Work*, he condemned what he described as "subtle methods of
job discrimination against Jews."[17]
    In order to help alleviate the problem which
he frequently reported, Marciniak aligned the CLA
with the B'nai B'rith Anti-Defamation League, and
the Alliance became instrumental in opening com-
munication between the League and other Catholic
groups. The CLA also provided speakers to
Catholic groups who urged them to reject the
simplistic and erroneous explanations of history
given by anti-Semetic speakers who traced all the
world's problems to Israel.
    The cause of racial and social justice was
still a difficult and unrewarding course to pursue in the forties and fifties and Marciniak was
branded a troublemaker and a Communist even by
people within his own religion who should have
known better. One reader advised Marciniak that
almost every Sunday the pastor of his Church

----

[15]Osborne, *Segregated Covenant*, pp.220-221.

[16]*Work,* November 1944.

[17]Ibid., October 1944.

railed from the pulpit against the editorial policies of *Work.* "The cause of today's trouble and unrest" the priest told his congregation was, "the fact that we are going against God." The priest warned that "God decreed the segregation of the races but man had gone against this". He condemned the editor of *Work* and others like him who were "trying to make the rest of us suffer from a malodorous, filthy, theiving race."[18]

Elizabeth Dilling, who headed a quasi-fascist group with the dubious name of "Patriotic Research Bureau", declared that the editor of *Work* had proved himself to be a Communist by "upholding the Red-backed C.I.O. . . .editorially opposing a ban on the Communist party. . . [and] praising socialist cooperatives".[19]

But Marciniak also began to receive important support and recognition in those days and he was one of the pioneers who raised the banner of Catholicism in the struggle for social justice in the city of Chicago. The Rosenwald Foundation which usually only contributed funds for black education in the South awarded a grant to the Catolic Labor Alliance for educating workers in an attempt to develop racial harmony in Chicago. The administrators of the fund stated that because of the Alliance's "excellent work" the foundation "stepped out of its usual policy in making a contribution".[20]

Dorothy Day visited Chicago and spoke at the Alliance's Labor School. Reporting her trip in the *Catholic Worker* she praised Marciniak's work. Pointing out that he had been a founder of the Catholic Worker in Chicago, she urged readers to subscribe to his new publication.[21]

From an Army Air Force base John Cogley wrote to Marciniak and congratulated him on his

---

[18]Ibid., November 1944.

[19]Gavagan, "Five Years of Work," p.14.

[20]Moly, "The CLA," p.28.

[21]*Catholic Worker*, November 1944.

new venture. He also asked if he could contribute an article to the new publication.[22] Marciniak enlisted the literary skill of his old
ally and in September, 1943 a column under
Cogley's name entitled, "Notes Along the Way"
began to appear. In it he attacked the segrga-
tion policies of most of Chicago's Catholic
institutions, and wrote eloquent arguments
against anti-Semitism. Cogley contributed a second column under the pseudonym Corporal John
Draftee in which he exprssed views on the post
war world. "Peace is not merely the absence of
war" he wrote, "but rather it is a normalization
of relationships between God and man and between
man and man." When he dreamt of peace, he said,
he thought of what "St. Augustine called the
'tranquility of order'. Peace can not be legis-
lated or decreed at a round table", he concluded,
peace "is the fruit of justice".[23]
        Marciniak maintained his own views of peace
in the paper also. He told Cogley that "other
members of the CLA were one hundred per cent
behind the war, and we don't see eye to eye on
the issue." But he stayed with them because "in
the greater view of things we are of one mind".[24]
Although he had complete control of the editorial
policies of the paper, he did not impose his
pacifism on it. He knew what that issue had done
to the New York Catholic Worker. But in subtle
ways he did explain his conscientious objection
to the war. In December 1944, when the issue of
peacetime conscription was being discussed, Marciniak called it dangerous, "because it put undo

---

[22]Cogley's letter to Marciniak is not in the
CLA files, but a copy of a letter Marciniak wrote
to Cogley August 15, 1943, acknowledges the good
wishes from Cogley and his request to write an
article.

[23]*Work*, September 1943.

[24]Marciniak to Cogley, August 15, 1943,
(CCWL File, Box 1)

emphasis on military might to solve world problems. International peace would only come," he
asserted, "when it is founded on law and justice.
To place our hope for peace in the military is to
destroy any chance of securing harmony and peace
among men."[25]

Although he had rejected conscription, Marciniak had discovered a way to work for peace.
And through the Catholic Labor Alliance he found
a way to pursue the goals he first outlined for
himself as a member of the Catholic Worker. In
pusuing these goals he also became the agent
through which the idealism of the Catholic Worker
went beyond the confines of the movement. Whereas
the radicalism of Dorothy Day kept the Catholic
Worker on the periphery of the Church in New
York, the liberalism of Marciniak brought the
fresh breath of spirit embodied by the Worker
movement into the mainstream of the Church in
Chicago.

---

[25]*Work*, December 1944.

CHAPTER XI

THE POST WAR YEARS

The war ended but it did not bring peace. The explosions in London, Dresden, Tokyo and Hiroshima had reverberated across the oceans and shaken the United States also. The world which American soldiers had left to defend had changed beyond recognition. Values and ideas had altered rapidly during the war years, and the perplexed soldier could waste little time evaluating these changes. All his energy was spent trying to absorb them.

Those who had run the Catholic Worker house on Blue Island Avenue before the war did not go back there, but rather began to plot new courses for their lives. Although they had abandoned the Worker movement, they had not forgotten the idealism which had initially drawn them to it and many of the former Catholic Workers pursued vocations in other forms of Catholic social action and journalism.

Despite the convolutons around him, John Cogley recalled the war years as the most uneventful period of his life. "It was a flop", he later wrote, "For all my vigorous anti-Nazism, I did almost nothing to defeat Hitler. Throughout the war I remained in an Army Air Force station in the United States. . .in utter safety and comparative comfort". As most Americans, he did spend a good deal of time dreaming of peace and the life he would have after the war ended.[1]

For Cogley, "returning to the Worker movement seemed out of the question." His family had grown to include a little boy and girl, and he had seen "too many families undergo unbearable strains due to their attempts to combine the routine of the Catholic Worker with family life."

---

[1]Cogley, *A Canterbury Tale*, p.36.

However he could not ignore the influence the Catholic Worker had on his life. Eventually he decided to start a publication which had a Catholic Worker perspective on contemporary issues. He shared his plan with Jim O'Gara, a former partner at the Catholic Worker house. O'Gara had run the house for a while and had been co-editor of the paper in its last year of publication.

The two men spent their last year in the service planning for the new publication. They foresaw it as a journal which would be an "up to the minute review of secular affairs as they affected the Catholic Community." Cogley envisioned a "kind of general version of the *Chicago Catholic Worker*". When both men returned to Chicago they prepared to implement their idea. As Cogley recalled, success seemed inevitable: "We were young and optimistic and we already had some experience". All they needed were the "funds to get the venture off the ground".[2] The best source of wealth they knew was Father H.A. Rinehold, a German refugee who had supported the Catholic Worker enthusiastically until the pacifist issue began to eclipse all others. From his parish in Seattle, Rinehold had become a well-known Catholic writer and the leading Catholic theorist on Church liturgy in the country.[3]

Rinehold had supported the *Chicago Catholic Worker* even after his split from the New York movement, and he continued to distribute it in Seattle until it ceased publication. When Cogley and O'Gara visited the priest with their new plan he was happy to help them. Through a wealthy friend, the priest secured a donation of a thousand dollars which served as seed money for the

---

[2]Ibid., p.36-37; also Jim O'Gara interview.

[3]Rodger Van Allen, *The Commonweal and American Catholicism* (Philadelphia: Fortress Press, 1974), p.106; Cogley, *Catholic America*, p.106.

new project. They used this gift to travel to New
York to meet "Father Rinehold's *really* rich
friends for more funds".[4]

In New York they visited townhouses, Wall
Street offices, and in general "saw wealth on a
scale to which they were not accustomed." While
visitng one place O'Gara remembered being told,
"Tomorrow we're going to take you to where the
real Catholic money is." But then came the warnings: "Downplay your interest in the racial question" and "be careful not to appear too pro-
labor, or too liberal." Disconcerted, but
nevertheless willing, the two men proceeded to
meet the "real wealth" of American Catholicism.
But, as Cogley remembered, "We kept giving the
wrong answers about racist practices, union
organizations and the social effects of our commitment to Roman Catholicism." [5] The men left
New York with their ideals intact, but their
funds exhausted.

On returning to Chicago they related their
experience to Father Martin Carrabine, and old
friend of the Catholic Worker. Carrabine suggested that they alter their proposed format
slightly and present the magazine under the
auspices of CISCA the Catholic youth group which
he still directed. He promised to give them complete editorial freedom and they accepted his
offer. With money from CISCA and a few rich
Catholics whom Carrabine knew, O'Gara and Cogley
began their publication which they called *Today.*

The magazine was supposed to be directed to
Catholic high school students, but its content
attracted a much wider audience. "It seemed to
some of our readers", Cogley later wrote, "that
we were shockingly contemporary and youthfully
impious." In *Today* they took up "social crusades"
and "wars against sentimentality in religion", as

---

[4]Van Allen, *Commonweal,* p.106; Cogley, *A
Canterbury Tale*, p. 37.

[5]Van Allen, *Commonweal*, p.106; Cogley, *A
Canterbury Tale,*p.37; O'Gara interview.

well as "satiric attacks on advertising, book
clubs, television and other popular pre-
occupations."[6]

For three years Cogley and O'Gara published
this magazine bi-monthly, and when they left it
was well on its way to becoming an important
national Catholic publication. Changing editors
and format a number of times, *Today* continued
until 1971, when under the direction of the
Ligourian Fathers it finally ceased publication.
In 1948 Cogley completed his college education
which he had begun a decade earlier, and left
Chicago to study Thomistic philosophy at the
University of Fribourg in Switzerland.[7] Shortly
after Cogley's departure, O'Gara also left the
magazine to do graduate work in sociology at
Loyola University of Chicago. During this time
in order to augment their income from the G.I.
Bill, O'Gara and Cogley both began writing arti-
cles for *Commonweal* and *America* the two leading
Catholic journals in the country.

O'Gara's articles dealt primarily with the
Chicago scene. In addition to comments on city
politics, he jabbed at the social conscience of
Catholics in Chicago. Reporting on skid row in
Chicago, an area he knew well from his days at
the Catholic Worker, he commented on the lack of
Catholics in the area performing works of mercy.
On the positive side, he also attracted attention
to the new spirit of social action which was
emerging in the Church in Chicago. Reporting on
the Sheil School of Social Studies in *America*, he
pointed out that the "school had over two thousand students" and had become a place "where

---

[6]Cogley, *A Canterbury Tale*, p.39.

[7]Ibid., p.39.

Catholics can meet, exchange ideas and acquire new ones."[8]

O'Gara established a reputation as a good writer and journalist, and after leaving Loyola he was asked to become editor of *St. Jude Messenger* in order to revive it. Under his direction, this magazine became the *Voice of St. Jude* and O'Gara transformed it from an overly pietistic Catholic family magazine into an up-to-date journal which dealt with secular affairs and their relation to Catholics.[9]

In 1949 Cogley returned from Europe and *Commonweal* editor, Ed Skillin offered him a position on his staff. Cogley first became feature editor, and when he was promoted to executive editor in 1952, he invited O'Gara to New York to become managing editor of *Commonweal*.

According to historian Rodger Van Allen, the appearance of the two former Catholic Workers "marked the emergence of a grass roots intellectuality for American Catholics and a discernible new development in *Commonweal's* history."[10] During this period the magazine became a forum for a small but growing minority within the Church whom Cogley described as "Catholic eggheads". Like their non-Catholic counterparts, this group believed that the Church's institutions, just as the government's, were being held captive by reactionaries. But they affirmed that

---

[8]James O'Gara, "Chicago's Misery Mile," *Commonweal* 50 (September 30, 1949): pp.598-600; "Chicago's Times Square," *America* 82 (January 28, 1950) : pp. 492-451; other O'Gara articles during this period include: "Divided City," *Commonweal* 51 (May 6, 1949): pp.86-89; "Stevenson and Kennelly," *Commonweal* 51 (December 23, 1949) : pp.313-315; "What Price Anti-Sedition?" *Commonweal* 50 (July 8, 1949): pp.312-315.

[9]Van Allen, *Commonweal*, p.107; O'Gara interview.

[10]Van Allen, *Commonweal*, p.107.

inherent in Canon Law, just as in the Constitu-
tion, a spirit of progress and liberty exisited
which needed to be expressed and defended.[11]
Therefore when a group of Catholics picketed the
Metropolitan Opera House because a priest was
shown in a bad light, the editors of *Commonweal*
stated that the protest was not merely silly, but
a perversion of Catholicism, since the Church had
always placed emphasis on the arts in its teachings.

With Cogley and O'Gara at the helm, *Commonweal* reflected and also attracted ideas which
had been characteristically part of the Catholic
Worker movement. As Marciniak, Cogley and O'Gara
represented the infusion of Catholic Worker radicalism into mainstream American Catholicism.
Historian David O'Brien has pointed out, in the
1950's "Cogley's *Commonweal* was regarded
accurately as a truly radical voice within the
Church".[12] According to Cogley, the editors
attempted to "take those values which are
American values--e.g. civil liberties, the Bill
of Rights, the separation of Church and State--
and offer a rationale for them which would be
comfortable to Catholic doctrine."[13]

Although their contemporaries described them
as radicals, the *Commonweal* editors were, by
Cogley's own admission, decidedly more in line
with the traditional liberal camp. Unlike the
Catholic Worker from where their politics sprang,
they accepted basic American institutions. If
Cogley was at all unconventional, it was in his
attempts to amalgamate Catholic thought to the

---

[11]John Cogley, "Catholic Eggheads," *Commonweal* 57 (December 19, 1952): p.274.

[12]David O'Brien, *The Renewal of American
Catholicism*, (New York: Oxford Press, 1972),
p.161.

[13]John Cogley, "Looking Backward Looking
Ahead: Fortieth Anniversary Symposium," *Commonweal* 81 (November 20, 1964): p.264.

broader tradition of American liberalism. And in this he was not revolutionary but rather anticipatory. For in a few years, America would elect an American Catholic liberal as president, and the argument at least as old as the nine-teenth century thought of Orestes Brownson and Isaac Hecker would be over.

Although the leading Catholic liberal in the country, Cogley never forgot his intellectual debt to the radicalism of the Catholic Worker.[14] Despite differences, he never criticized Dorothy Day in print, in fact he came to recognize and acknowledge the intellectual debt he owed the movement and was not afraid to defend the Worker in print during a period when it would have been convenient to forget radical idealism. Although he was decidedly not a pacifist, Cogley defended the pacifism of the Worker. In an article in 1953 he wrote, "Please God that there will always be pacifists around to ask [hard questions] . The witness of pacifists bespeaks doubts that might otherwise be silenced by the rest of us, and without doubts I think we are all lost."[15]

Although he was writing about pacifism, Cogley nurtured his doubts on other issues as well. He did not share the blind faith in material progress of many of his liberal con-temporaries. He also maintained a healthy cynicism of the American system that many of his coreligionists were so eager to absorb. He had spent too many sleepless nights listening to the sobs of the destitute, he had dealt with too many government bureaucrats while directing the Catholic Worker house to believe that good faith

---

[14] Mel Piehl has also noted the contrast between the radical roots of Cogley and his later liberalism; see: *Breaking Bread: The Catholic Worker and the Origin of Catholic Radicalism in America* (Philadelphia: Temple University Press, 1982), pp. 170-172.

[15] John Cogley, "Pacifists", *Commonweal* 59 (October 23, 1953): p.54.

and good government would eventually lead to a gentle harmony in American life. It would be too facile to simply describe Cogley as a liberal in the mold of the 1950's. His experience at the Catholic Worker to which he frequently referred, does not allow it.

Cogley had written his article on pacifism for an American public that had purchased over three million copies of Mickey Spillane's *One Lonely Night*.[16] The hero of the novel, Mike Hammer, bragged, "I killed more people tonight than I have fingers on my hands. I shot them in cold blood and enjoyed every moment of it. . . . They were commies Lee. They were red sons of bitches who should have died long ago. . . . They never thought there were people like me in this country. They figured us all to be soft as horse manure and just as stupid".

The war, the bomb, Communism, and Arnold Toynbee all told Americans what many of them had been suspecting for a long time. Their civilization was being threatened. Materially, the average American was better off than he had ever been. Fred Vinson, director of war mobilization and reconversion reported that "the American people live in the pleasant predicament of having to learn to live fifty per cent better than they have ever lived before". [17]

Nevertheless something was missing. In Cleveland, editorialist Louis Seltzer lamented, "We have everything. We are, on the average, rich beyond the kings of old. . . yet. . . something is not there that should be-- something we once had."[18] In vain, Americans searched for an idea or myth to guide them into the second half of an uncertain century. As waves on a shoreline

---

[16]Eric Goldman, *The Crucial Decade* (New York: Alfred Knopf, 1956), p.211.

[17]Ibid., p.14.

[18]"The Long Road," *Commonweal* 52 (June 2, 1959): pp. 187-188.

heroes rapidly rose and fell just as quickly.
Mac Arthur faded noisily but nevertheless he
faded. For a while religion came into vogue (even
Mickey Spillane joined a church). But the most
dangerous of all these trends occured when
mediocrity and Americanism became a cult and
Joseph Mc Carthy led the campaign against those
who would not join.

The most important campaign that Cogley took
up while editor of *Commonweal* was his clash with
Joseph Mc Carthy. As he had done a decade and a
half earlier against Coughlinism, Cogley now
launched a journalistic attack on Mc Carthyism
while most writers remained timid observers of
the phenomenon. In June 1950, the *Commonweal* in
a lead editorial referred to Mc Carthy as a
"reckless bogeyman." This began a four-year
campaign against the Senator during which Cogley
became "the most articulate anti-Mc Carthy
Catholic in the country".[19]

Aside from the *Catholic Worker, Commonweal*
was the only major Catholic journal to consistently oppose the politics of Joseph Mc
Carthy. At the crest of his influence in early
1954, a Gallup poll reported that 58 per cent of
the Catholics in the country supported Mc
Carthy.[20] This represented a substantial majority
but it did not reflect the degree to which the
Catholic press rallied to the Senator.

Many Catholic editors embraced McCarthyism
as a sign of patriotism. They were quick to
point out the Catholicism of Mc Carthy and that
their Church had been consistent in its opposition to Communism and had even condemned it when
many Americans had been duped into becoming
"fellow-travellers" in the thirties and
forties.[21]

The Catholic magazine *Sign* stated that Mc
Carthy had "stumbled upon the leftist nest in a

---

[19]Van Allen, *Commonweal*, p.111.

[20]Cogley, *Catholic America*, p.112.

[21]Ibid., p.113.

speech . . .and ever since has doggedly tried to carry through the unmasking of Leftists in the State department."[22] Another Catholic magazine defended Mc Carthy for fighting Communism "the way you fight rattlesnakes; without a rulebook. *"The Brooklyn Tablet*, which had defended Coughlinism in the late thirties, frequently published letters praising McCarthy. One reader wrote, "McCarthyism to me is one hundred percent anti-Communism, I glory in my McCarthyism."[23]

As he had done while editor of the *Chicago Catholic Worker*, Cogley condemned this crude form of anti-Communism. He knew that Communism was too dynamic to be thwarted by speeches and meetings. Borrowing from his Catholic Worker memories he wrote the problem with Catholics is that they "gave too much to the anti-Communist crusade and not enough to Christianity." But few Catholics were willing to heed Cogley's criticism, for what he had observed in the thirties was even more true in the affluent fifties. Catholics, along with most other Americans, were enjoying life too much to be troubled by the problems of the poor that remained.

The most important contribution Cogley made during the McCarthy era was when he wrote a speech for his old friend Bishop Sheil of Chicago. Sheil was the only member of the Catholic hierarchy to condemn the Senator and during a week when Cardinal Spellman had shaken McCarthy's hand and praised him for his anti-Communism, Sheil read a Cogley-written speech which chastised McCarthy. Addressing 2500 auto workers Sheil said that the time had come to cry out against "the phony anti-Communism that flouts our traditions and democratic procedures, and sense of fair play." True anti-Communism, Sheil explained, meant being interested "in such mat-

---

[22]"Mc Carthy, Mac Arthur, and Mc Carran," *Sign* 31 (October, 1951): p.6.

[23]*The Brooklyn Tablet*, August 30, 1952.

ters as seeing to it that people get enough to eat, have decent homes, and are able to raise their children in dignity."[24]

McCarthy's response to Cogley was sharp. "I feel you have done and are doing a tremendous disservice to the Catholic Church", he wrote, and warned him that *Commonweal* magazine which was "falsely and dishonestly masquerading as a mouthpiece for the Catholic Church" was contributing "unlimited service to the Communist movement". The editors of *Commonweal* responded to McCarthy's attacks by stating that they were pleased their magazine was included on the roster of McCarthy's enemies.[25] Together the former Catholic Workers from Chicago, Cogley and O'Gara set the tone for *Commonweal* and it became as David O'Brien has pointed out, the leader of "Catholic liberalism and the voice of the educated, articulate, Americanized Catholic layman."[26]

While pursuing their new vocations after the war, Cogley and O'Gara both leaders in the early Catholic Worker movement, maintained at least intellectually their close connection with the movement. Shortly before joining the staff at *Commonweal*, Cogley wrote an article for the New York *Catholic Worker* on the occasion of its fifteenth anniversary. "Because I was one of the ones whc was profoundly affected by the Catholic Worker, because it has meant so much to me in my life and work", he confessed that to try to reflect on what the "movement and its leaders have meant to the Church in America" found him "deeply stirred and anxious to express gratitude to the Providence which directed them."

When Cogley began writing for *Commonweal*, the Catholic Worker movement had turned fifteen years old, but its impact on American Catholicism

---

[24]Van Allen, *Commonweal*,p.114.

[25]James O'Gara, "McCarthy the Case Against Him," *Commonweal* 57 (October 31, 1952): p. 95.

[26]O'Brien, *American Catholicism*, p.160.

was just beginning to be felt. Graduates of the movement's first generation were just beginning to introduce the basic ideals of the Catholic Worker to a larger cross section of the Catholic community. In 1952, Dwight MacDonald noted that "many individuals who are now working. . . in strange Catholic vineyards were given their first impulse and their training in the Catholic Worker movement."[27] One example of McDonald's observation was the work Cogley and O'Gara were doing at *Commonweal*, as they transformed that journal into an intellectual offshoot of the Catholic Worker.[28]

In actuality however they had left the Worker movement. Despite their intellectual allegiance, they no longer lived in voluntary poverty, sheltering the homeless and feeding the hungry. Tom Sullivan another former member of the Chicago Catholic Worker did return to that special calling. In 1938 shortly after their friend, Al Reser had married, Cogley, Sullivan and a few others at the Catholic Worker stood outside the house on Blue Island Avenue and discussed the possiblities of their own futures and whom they might marry. Sullivan spread his arms out toward the Catholic Worker house and exclaimed, "This shall be my bride!"[29]

---

[27]Dwight MacDonald "Foolish Things of the World," *New Yorker* (October 11, 1952): p. 37.

[28]*Commonweal* was just one of many Catholic journals influenced by the Catholic Worker. As historian William Miller has pointed out, "For Catholics the time just after the war was one of seeming progress. . . . The relationship of the Worker movement to this new spirit of confidence . . .was indicated in part by the new publications begun by persons associated with the movement. Among those were *Work, Today,* [and] *Integrity*. Miller, *Harsh and Dreadful Love*, p.217.

[29]Sullivan interview; O'Gara interview.

His assertion in a moment of levity proved close to the truth. After the war he visited Dorothy Day in New York City. He planned a short visit, but he stayed for almost ten years, the longest anyone has run the New York house of hospitality. He told a reporter years later, "The place was a mess, of course I had to pitch in and clean it up. After that I was hooked."[30]

The Catholic Worker house had undergone a great transformation. It was but a skeleton of the vibrant movement it had been. The house was occupied solely by the indigent. In 1948 John Cogley had spoken of the movement in terms of the past. "Now there are only seven or eight houses left", he wrote in *America* magazine. In response Dorothy Day commented, "Yes the problems have become intensified. A great many have left the running. Where there were thirty-two houses and farms now there are eleven." But, she pointed out, "In those eleven we are still trying to work out a theory of love so that the revolution of love instead of hate may come about."[31]

House counting was not the basis on which the movement should be judged. John Cogley wrote many years later that it disturbed Dorothy Day that the charitable work of the movement was taken more seriously than the ideas presented in the paper. The thought escaped most people that the works of mercy performed at the Catholic Worker were a reflection of the ideas which the movement professed.

It was a good time for Sullivan to move into the house of hospitality in New York. His humor and wit were probably good antidotes for the troubled times. One of his favorite pastimes when he was not warding off bill collectors was challenging pacifists who congregated at the house. "There I was for years in the Pacific fighting to protect you lousy C.O.'s", he used to

---

[30]Mc Donald, "Foolish Things of the World," p.58.

[31]*Catholic Worker*, September, 1942.

complain. Although these arguments often began as harmless banter, Dorothy Day recalled that they often degenerated into "quiet but venomous words." [32]

Sullivan wrote a column for the *Catholic Worker* entitled "Mott Street". This column became "Chrystie Street" when the Catholic Workers moved there in 1950. He reported day by day occurences around the house in such a manner as to make people believe that there was a quiet joy in voluntary poverty. "We had a dignified lady join us for dinner one night", he told readers. After she ate she went to the kitchen and announced to the helpers there, "I am not thanking you bums for a bit of the meal I just ate", and pointing to the crucifix on the kitchen wall she declared, "I am thanking the man on the cross".[33]

Aside from the ever present poor, there were fewer visitors to the Catholic Worker in the forties and fifties, and those that did come were different. In the thirties, the visitors typified their generation. The small group that came in the fifties were misfits. They remained unimpressed with their country's newly acquired affluence and influence in the world. And their troubling over the bomb went deeper than the fear that it might be used on their country. They did not like the Communists either, but not because of McCarthy's ravings but because of events such as the Hitler-Stalin pact and the murder of Trotsky.

Representative of this new group that found their way to the lower east side of New York was Michael Harrington. A refugee from the Midwest, he worked for a while on a magazine in Greenwich Village and eventually found his way to the Worker house. Sullivan recalled the first day Harrington arrived. He invited the young man in

---

[32]Dorothy Day, *Loaves and Fishes* (New York: Curtiss Publishers, 1972), p.136.

[33]*Catholic Worker*, October 1952.

and asked if he would help to wrap bundles of the paper. Harrington moved into the house where he wrote for the paper and helped on the soupline for two years. In the introduction to his powerfully influential book, *The Other America*, he wrote, "It was through Dorothy Day and the Catholic Worker movement that I first came into contact with the terrible reality of involuntary poverty and the magnificent idea of voluntary poverty."[34]

The writer Dwight McDonald also visited the Worker house frequently in the early 1950's and became convinced that the Worker movement would provide good material for a book or at least a series of articles. He proposed his idea to *New Yorker* magazine and received an advance for the project. Tom Sullivan was immediately suspicious and vented his feelings in his column in the *Catholic Worker*. He was concerned what the *New Yorker* could do to a person or institution. A native Chicagoan, Sullivan recalled what the magazine had done to his hometown. After they finished tearing Chicago down, he commented, "I got the impression that there was less left than after the fire".[35] But when McDonald's articles began to appear in the magazine, even Sullivan had to admit that "they were pretty fair pieces of writing".

Many readers of the *Catholic Worker* were not as pleased. One person wrote to say that it was a terrible mistake for the Catholic Worker to become involved with a magazine that was such an "outstanding source of nourishment for the bourgeois mind."[36] But no one would leave the Worker over such a trivial issue; there were so few places to go.

---

[34]Michael Harrington, *The Other America* (New York: MacMillan and Co.,1972), p.vii; see also Piehl, *Breaking Bread*, pp. 173-177.

[35]*Catholic Worker,*October 1952.

[36]Ibid.

In 1953 the flames which McCarthy and others had been fannning burst into one gigantic explosion. A series of events which began with the arrest of a scientist in England rapidly centered around a Jewish television repairman and his wife. Dorothy Day recalled the day June 19, 1953, that Julius and Ethel Rosenberg walked to the death chamber. "That June evening the air was fresh with honeysuckle. Out under the hedge. . .the black cat played with a grass snake, and the newly cut grass was fragrant in the evening air." She noted that Ethel Rosenberg's last gesture was to kiss one of the police matrons who accompanied her to the death chair. "Her last gesture was a gesture of love", Dorothy wrote, "Let us have no part in the vindictive state and let us pray for Ethel and Julius Rosenberg."

The fifties were difficult times for those who did not glory in the prospect of being "an average American". In Chicago, however, Ed Marciniak had fared better than most of his fellow reformers. He continued to publish *Work*, and in the fifties it became one of the most important labor papers in the country. His work as spokesman for labor won for him a position on the delegation representing the United States at the Forty-Third International Labor Conference at Geneva, Switzerland. Monsignor George Higgins, who had succeeded John Ryan as head of the Social Action Department of the National Catholic Welfare Conference, praised the selection of Marciniak. He called the appointment appropriate since "there were few labor leaders and few American Catholic social actionists who have done more than he to popularize the philosophy underlying [the goals of the convention]."[37]

During the fifties, Marciniak had become vice president of the Newspaper guild, a board member of the housing conference of Chicago, a member of the Catholic Interracial Council, the

---

[37]N.C.W.C. news release, June 27, 1959, Marciniak Papers.

Chicago Council against Discrimination, and the
Chicago Commission on Human Relations.[38]
     In 1960 when he was appointed Director of
the Commission on Human Relations, the con-
gratulatory letters he received read like a history of his accomplishments in the area of social
action. Among others letters of congratulations
came from B'nai B'rith Anti-Defamation League,
the *Chicago Defender* and the Chicago Interracial
Council. When asked if his lofty position would
become more of a handicap than an asset to his
activism, Marciniak replied, "I think I am the
same guy playing a different role. It's the
nature of the political process that you engage
in a sort of give and take to get things done.
But let me emphasize, that this way you do get
things done." [39]
     The liberal Catholic agenda could not be
more succinctly defined. Dorothy Day's
uncompromising radicalism may remain as an ideal,
but for her proteges it was more important to
utilize the model to some practical end. Marciniak exemplified the best of many former
Catholic Workers who had been touched by the
movement's idealism before journeying into other
fields of action. Dorothy Day stated that spending time with the Catholic Worker gave many young
people a springboard for professional work in
their chosen careers. "Social Work, editing,
labor organizing, teaching, writing, nursing-- in
all these fields", she pointed out, "there are
Catholic Workers". [40] This assertion was particularly true of the those who started the movement in Chicago. Some like Marciniak, Cogley and
O'Gara became famous. Others like Marty Paul who

---

[38]"He Works for a Living," *Sign* 33 (January,
1955): p.34.

[39]Bruce Cook, "Outsider on the Inside,"
National Catholic Reporter (January 20, 1965):
p.2.

[40]Day, *Loaves and Fishes*, p. 132.

re-established his farm commune after the war were not so well known. Nevertheless all remained committed to the ideals they had out-lined for themselves in the late thirties on Blue Island Avenue.

The Catholic Worker idea continued, but in Chicago in the fifites the movement was all but non-existent. All that remained was the original house on Taylor Street, the place where Mar-ciniak, Cogley and the others had first discov-ered and discussed the movement. The Taylor Street house was but a remnant of the spirited pre-war days. John Bowers had kept the house going long after everyone had departed, and transformed it into a neighborhood gathering place for the local children. The brash man in dandified dress who had shocked many with his flippant remarks was now a quiet man in worn clo-thing, indistinguishable from those he helped. Living midst cobwebs and dust, his tattered con-dition symbolized the passing of an era.

In January 1950, Bowers died and with him passed all evidence of a once vibrant movement. Tom Sullivan wrote Bowers' obituary in the *Catholic Worker* and related to readers across the country the work the man had done in Chicago. Dorothy Day travelled to Chicago for the funeral and wrote in her column, "I remember something he had done for me years ago when I was taken ill in Chicago and paid not only for my hospital bill. . . . but for the operation on my throat. He was a man of taste and culture" , she wrote, "May God grant him a place of refreshment, light and peace."

Shortly after Bowers' death, another group began a Catholic Worker house in Chicago. "Our house is located slightly south of the Loop" Fred O'Connell wrote to Dorothy Day. He told her that they slept thirty men every night in their house of hospitality and every day they took a truck-load of food down to Madison Avenue. There they distributed "ten gallons of soup and all the bread the men want".[41]

---

[41]*Catholic Worker*, June, 1950.

CHAPTER XII

THE WORD MADE FLESH

"Many people are beginning to speak of the Catholic Worker in the past tense", Dorothy Day wrote in September 1948. She was responding to a comment made by John Cogley in *Commonweal.* Cogley may not have been far off the mark. In the 1950's the people of the United States seemed to take a deep collective sigh of relief and fall into a much needed slumber. Social upheaval was in the past and the embourgeoisment of America began anew. Peace was at hand, Europe had been saved, and the Communists had been checked in Greece and Korea. It was time to relax from the tumultuous thirties and forties and enjoy the affluence of the fifties. Those who at one time had read the *Catholic Worker* and supported the movement, preferred to ignore the issues it continued to raise and tried to forget their former proximity to problems of unemployment, foreclosures and war.

Periodically there were reports in the New York *Catholic Worker* that a new house had opened in Chicago. This might have heartened Dorothy Day, but it probably also caused a little melancholia. She no doubt felt that despite the good intentions of these newcomers, they would never match the work done by the young idealists who undertook a similar mission in the thirties. But like the monks of early medieval Europe, the new group, propelled by the energy of their predecessors, preserved the idea of the Catholic Worker.

In the 1960's the torch passed to a new generation of Catholic Workers at precisely the same moment that events began to stir the country from its somnolence. As new groups of unorganized workers such as farm laborers sought union representation, a new group of Catholics discovered a philosophy of labor within the pages of the *Catholic Worker.* As the struggle for civil rights intensified, the Catholic Worker's traditional

171

view on racism became relevant once more.
Finally and most importantly, when the issue of
war and peace took precedence over all others,
Catholics discovered in the Worker history a
tradition of non-violence. Long before the first
bishops letter on the legitimacy of the conscientious objector position appeared in November
1968, the Catholic Worker had provided support
for those Catholics who refused to participate in
the Vietnam War. Ironically, pacifism, the issue
which almost buried the Catholic Worker in the
forties was the central force behind its
revitalization in the sixties as Catholics numbered the greatest number of religious objectors
in the country. Indicative of this resurrection
in Chicago was the emergence of Karl Meyer as the
dominant force in the Catholic Worker movement
there. Meyer, a pacifist and a convert to
Catholicism, used a Cathoic Worker house which he
started as a base for his pacifist activities
which were national in scope, and he used the
Catholic Worker as a sounding board for his
ideas. Throughout the sixties and seventies
Meyer became a nationally recognized leader of
the peace movement. He organized pickets at
military installations, joined the much heralded
march to Moscow in 1961, travelled to Vietnam in
1965, and spearheaded the tax resistor movement
against military spending. The activites of
people such as Meyer in newly established
Catholic Worker houses across the country
attracted renewed attention to a movement that
most thought had succumbed to the temper of the
times. Although in the sixties the Worker movement did not regain the appeal that it once
enjoyed among the general populace of the Church,
it became a giant among Catholic intellectuals.

As nuclear proliferation and the war in
Vietnam intensified, making an ugly caracature of
the United States' self imposed role of
peacekeeper, Catholic intellectuals found within
the pages of the *Catholic Worker* a theology of
peace. Historians also began to recognize the
significance of the Worker movement of the

thirties when the neophyte Catholic Workers of that era began to take roles of leadership in the Church of the sixties and began to direct the attention of the Church hierarchy toward issues of peace and social justice.

Those who rediscvered the Catholic Worker in the 1960's also found within the movement responses to other problems that plagued their troubled decade. When farmworkers began their struggle for union recognition and sought the Church as an ally, the Catholic Worker rallied to their cause and this time, with the help of Catholic intellectuals, many who were former Catholic Workers, brought the bishops along with them. Today the words "peace and justice' ring like an anthem for a morally revitalized Catholic Church. But as the leaders of the Church crusade for social, political and economic justice they are treading ground already plotted by young idealists of the 1930's and forties who called themselves Catholic Workers. In the 1950's material progress seemed to mock the Worker movement, but history has since justified it.

As it gained notoriety, scholars began asking questions about the Catholic Worker. What made this movement, started by a convert, an immigrant and Catholic students so prophetic? They debated the "peculiar synthesis" of Peter Maurin's communitarian Catholicism and Dorothy Day's latent socialism. To many, the significance of the Worker became simply, the ideas of the movement, but it was more than that, it was an idea made flesh.

What is the Catholic Worker? It depends on who is answering the question. To the unemployed worker it is a dry bed and a cup of soup. To the scholar it is an idea, an interesting synthesis of Catholicism, utopian socialism and pacifism. To those of a subtler mind it is an attempt to remythologize the historic church to give it a greater contemporary significance. The Catholic Worker is more than this. A Catholic could describe the movement as a holy apparition rising out of human frailty. The historic Catholic

Worker movement was people who came together and acted in the image of Christ. When they fed the poor, they were with Christ of the Sermon on the Mount.   When they argued over issues such as pacifism, they were with Christ who argued in the temple with the rabbis.   And when they were simply enjoying the community that a shared vision evokes, they were with Christ in the company of his friends, the Apostles. The Catholic Workers of the thirties and forties became the model for the institutional Church of the decades that followed, and for this the American Catholic Church owes a great debt to the Marciniak's, Cogley's and O'Gara's and other Catholic Worker pioneers who carried the idea of the movement beyond the shelter of their storefront hospices.

When placed in the context of American intellectual history, The Catholic Worker has been described as spiritual, anti-materialistic, and even overly idealistic.   But another adjective is needed to complete this description. That is, the movement was instinctual.   It developed out of a basic urge to community. Events and ideas of the eighteenth and nineteenth centuries had eroded tradtional forms of community which had been centuries in the making.   It is no coincidence that the Catholic Worker, despite its inclination toward utopian agrarianism, remained primarily an urban movement.   Besides the fact that most Catholics lived in the city, it was in urban America that the demise of traditional forms of community became most apparent.   Therefore the city produced the first solutions to the crisis.   By the end of the nineteenth century civic clubs and professional organizations proliferated.   They all owe there existence to nature's abhorence of vacuum.   The difficulty with these new manifestations of community was that they tended to be more exclusive than inclusive: the dentist could not join the A.M.A., a worker could not join the Rotarians, an Irishman could not join the Italian-American club, and blacks were excluded everywhere.   To those with a sense of humanity these groups denied the essential purpose of their existence. Even the Catholic Church, which boasted a tradition of community, failed to fulfill its historic purpose. During this era the Church took care of its own, building protective walls around its flock.

It is easy to understand why early Chicago Catholic Workers such as Cogley, Marciniak and Sullivan were seminary drop outs. In theory they felt that their Church could solve the crisis of community, but in reality they learned that most priests were not ready to open their spiritual arms. The nature of the Church is to be dynamic, it does not thrive in a stagnant or defensive posture. When the official Church does not fulfill its historic mission, the spirit which protects it provides other means. In the thirties this spirit provided the inspiration for the Catholic Worker movement.

Peter Maurin attracted idealists in Chicago as elsewhere because he elicited a new vision for the Church. His idea was Catholic which appealed to their intellect, and communal which appealed to their instincts. The pursuit of community in the thirties had reached demonic proportions, but the Catholic Worker did not contribute to these illusions. Whereas demogogues evoked a sense of community by appealing to the lowest common denominator, the Catholic Worker appealed to a spiritual denominator realized in the image of Christ. For many, even the symbol of Christ had become a divisive tool, but the Christ of the Catholic Worker was all inclusive. To the Jew he was the Christ of Jerusalem, to the worker he was the son of a carpenter, to the oppressed he was the author of the Sermon on the Mount. The Catholic Workers lived the communal truth of their Church. A phrase which appeared frequently in the *Chicago Catholic Worker* was the "Mystical Body of Christ". Devoid of its most subtle theological implications, to the Chicago Catholic Workers it simply meant that all were one in Christ. Therefore when the Jews were attacked by demagogues and gangs, the *Chicago Catholic Worker* reminded readers that "Spiritually we are all Semites". When workers were oppressed, they rallied to their cause, and finally when war threatened to tear the Mystical Body asunder, many became pacifists.

By embracing the image of Christ they accepted his central message which was to build the kingdom of God. In the Judeo-Christian tradition, building the kingdom of God had always been a central axiom to political and economic life. This maxim is at least as old as the Book of Exodus when God tells the Jews that "You shall be to me a priestly kingdom and a holy nation". And in a sense, it continued through to the eighteenth century as a justification for absolute monarchy. When, in the eighteenth century, the philosophes, as Carl Becker and others have pointed out, overthrew theology and created the earthly kingdom, they took western thought onto a new philosophic path. Although this new metaphysics was responsible for a tremendous surge of material progress, it caused disruptions in human relationships which have yet to be reconciled. By reaching into their intellectual and spiritual tradition, the Catholic Workers attempted to reestablish the sacred as a model for social order.

The Catholic hierarchy rose to the challenge created by the activists of the thirties, and by the 1980's, as Jay Dolan has pointed out, social activism has become the central issue of American Catholicism.[1] There are many factors involved in this ecclesiastical development, but a central cause is the influence of a small group of Catholic radicals in thirties who saw in the heritage of their religion a call to social justice.[2] The Marciniak's, O'Gara's and Meyer's who

---

[1]Dolan, *The American Catholic Experience*, p.452

[2]An excellent overview and analysis of the changing mind of the American Church appears in Dolan's *American Catholic Experience*, pp. 349-383.

were part of the Cathoic Worker in Chicago have
moved on into other dimensions of social
activism, but the movement continues to thrive in
Chicago because the words spoken in the parks and
churches of Chicago in the thirties still appeal
to those who see their religion as a quiet but
powerful force of community in a world moving
toward the opposite.

BIBLIOGRAPHY

MANUSCRIPT COLLECTIONS

Chicago, Illinois. Catholic Labor Alliance Papers, Chicago Historical Society Archives.

Chicago, Illinois. Arthur Falls Personal Papers.

Chicago, Illinois. Karl Meyer's Personal Papers.

Chicago, Illinois. Edward Marciniak Personal Papers, Loyola University Institute of Urban Studies.

Chicago, Illinois. Sheil School of Social Studies, Papers, Chicago Historical Society.

Milwaukee, Wisconsin. Catholic Worker-Dorothy Day Papers, Marquette University Archives.

Milwaukee, Wisconsin. Catholic Association for International Peace Collection, Marquette University Archives.

ARTICLES

Betten, Neil. "Urban Catholicism and Industrial Reform." *Thought* 44 (Fall, 1969): 434-450.

Blakly, Paul. "Labor Wages a Losing Battle." *America*, (February 6, 1937): 417-418

Boisen, Anton. "C.O.'s, Their Morale in Church Operated Service." *Psychiatry* 7 (May, 1944):222.

Breig, Joseph. "Apostle on the Bum." *Commonweal* (April 29, 1938): 9-12.

Breunig, Charles. "The Condemnation of the Sillon: An Episode in the History of the Christian Democracy in France." *Church History* 26 (September, 1957): 227-244.

"Catholic Stand on War." *Time* (November 23, 1942): 24.

"Catholic Students Are Against War." *Christian Century* (March 9, 1939).

"Clergy Poll." *Commonweal* (October 31, 1941):7.

"C.O.'s in Prison." *Christian Century* (March 8, 1944):302-304.

Cogley, John. "The Failure of Anti-Communism." *Commonweal*(July 21, 1950): 357-358.

_____. "Looking Backward, Looking Ahead, Fortieth Anniversary Symposium." *Commonweal* (November 20, 1964):4

_____. "Pacifists." *Commonweal*(October 23, 1953):54.

_____. "Storefront Catholicism." *America*(August 21, 1948):447-449.

Cook, Bruce. "Outsider on the Inside." *National Catholic Reporter* (January 20, 1965):2.

Cort, John. "The Charms of Anarchism." *Commonweal* (November 14, 1952): 139-140.

_____. "Catholics in Trade Unions." *Commonweal* (May 5, 1939): 34-36.

Day, Dorothy. "It was a Good Dinner." *Commonweal* (August 23, 1940): 364-365.

Bibliography

    _____. 'Peter the Agitator." *Black Friars* (September 1949) :409-415.

    Falls, Arthur. "Catholic Obligation to Fight Racism." *Interracial Review* (October, 1933) 184.

    Ferkiss, Victor. "Populist Influences on American Fascism." *Western Political Quarterly*10 (June, 1957): 350-373.

    Fichter, John. "Labor Wages a Losing Battle." *America*(February 6, 1937): 562-572.

    Furfey, Paul Hanley. "The Layman in the Church." *Commonweal* (June 2, 1950): 123-125.

    Gleason, Philip. "In Search of a Unity: American Catholic Thought, 1920-1960." *Catholic Historic Review*65 (April 197): 185-205.

    Hellman, John. "The Opening of the left in French Catholicism: The Role of the Personalists." *Journal of the History of Ideas*34 (July 1973): 381-390.

    "He Works for a Living." *Sign* (January 1955): 34.

    Ley, Harold. "Catholicism and the Negro." *Christian Century.* (December 20, 1944):1476-79.

    "Long Road, The." *Commonweal*(June 2, 1950): 187-188.

    Lucey, Robert J. "Labor in Recession." *Commonweal* (May 6, 1938): 47.

    "McCarthy, MacArthur, McCarran." *Sign*, (October 1951): 6.

    Mc Carthy, Joseph. "Senator McCarthy Replies." *Commonweal* (November 27, 1953): 190.

Mc Donald, Dwight. "Foolish Things of the World." *New Yorker*, October 4-11, 1952.

McDonald, Dwight. "Why Politics?" *Politics* 1 (February 1945):6-8.

McNeal, Patricia. "Catholic Conscientious Objection During World War II." *Catholic Historical Review* 61 (April 1975):219-231.

Marciniak, Ed. "Catholic Social Doctrine and the Layman." *America* (February 7, 1959)

_____. "Constancy to the Church and Social Teaching."*America*(November 11, 1972): 393.

Maynard, Thomas. "Catholics and Nazis." *American Mercury*, (October 1941):391-400.

"Methods, The." *Ave Maria*(January 1954):6.

Michel, Virgil. "Personality and Liturgy." *Oratre Fratres*(February 19, 1938): 156-159.

O'Gara, James. "What Price Sedition?" *Commonweal*(July 8, 1949):312-315.

_____. "Stevenson and Kennelly." *Commonweal*(December 23, 1949): 313-315.

_____. "Divided City." *Commonweal*(May 6, 1949): 86-89.

_____. "Chicago's Times Square." *America*(January 28, 1950) 492-494.

_____. "Chicago's Misery Mile." *Commonweal*(September 30, 1949): 598-600.

_____. "Mc Carthy, the Case Against Him." *Commonweal* (October 31, 1952):95.

Parsons, Wilfred. "Can A Catholic Be a COnscientious Objector?" *Commonweal* (June 2, 1941):226.

Bibliography

Paul, Marty. "Diary of a Romantic Agrarian." *Commonweal*(January 2, 1953):327-330.

Roe, Walter. "Conscientious Objectors." *New Republic*(January 8, 1945):49.

Ryan, John A. "Sit Down Strike." *Ecclesiastical Review*(April 1937): 419-420.

Skillin, Ed. "Back of the Yards." *Commonweal*(November 29, 1940): 143-144.

Thompson, R.E.S. "Onward Christian Soldiers." *Saturday Evening Post*(August 16, 1941):53.

Weil, Simone. "Reflections on War." *Politics* 2 (February 1945): 54-55.

Zahn, Gordon. "Leaven of Love and Justice." *America*(November 11, 1972): 393.

BOOKS

Aaron, Daniel. *Writers on the Left*. New York:Harcourt Brace, 1963.

Abell, Aaron. *American Catholicism and Social Action: 1865-1950*. Garden City: Hanover House, 1960.

_____. *American Catholic Thought on Social Qiestions*. New York: Bobbs-Merrill, 1968.

Adams, Henry. *The Education of Henry Adams*.Boston: Houghton Mifflin Company, 1918.

Agar, Herbert. *Land of the Free.* Boston: Houghton Mifflin, 1918.

Allen, Frederick Lewis. *The Big Change: 1900-1950.* New York: Bantam Books, 1965.

American Jewish Committee. *Father Coughlin: His Arguments and His Facts.* New York: American Jewish Committee, 1939.

Bell, Daniel. *The Radical Right* Garden City: Doubleday and Co., 1961.

Berdyaev, Nicholas. *Slavery and Freedom.* New York: Charles Scribners and Sons, 1944.

Betten, Neil *Catholic Activism and the Industrial Worker.* Gainesville: University of Florida Press, 1976.

Bloy, Leon. *Pilgrim of the Absolute.* New York: Pantheon Books, 1947.

Broderick, Francis. *Right Reverend New Dealer John Ryan.* New York: MacMillan and Co., 1963.

Callahan, Daniel ed., *The Mind of the Catholic Layman.* New York: Sheed and Ward, 1963.

_____. *Generation of a Third Eye.* New York: Sheed and Ward, 1965.
Chatfield, Charles. *For Peace and Justice.* Knoxville: University of Tennessee Press, 1971.

Clancy, William, ed. *The Moral Dilemma of Nuclear Weapons.* New York: Church Peace Union, 1961.

Cogley, John. *A Canterbury Tale* New York: Seabury Press, 1976.

Bibliography

_____. *Catholic America.* Dial Press, 1973.

Coughlin, Charles, *Am I an Anti-Semite?*Detroit: Condon Press, 1939.

Day, Dorothy. *House of Hospitality* New York: Sheed and Ward, 1939.

_____. *Loaves and Fishes.* New York: Curtiss Books, 1972.

Derber, Milton and Young, Edward. *Labor and the New Deal.* Madison: University of Wisconsin Press, 1957.

Dolan, Jay. *The American Catholic Experience.* New York: Image Books, 1985.

Drake, St. Clair, and Clayton, Horace. *Black Metropolis: A Study of Negro Life in a Northern City.*New York: Harcourt Brace and World, Inc., 1945.

Drummond, Willaim. *Social Justice.* Milwaukee: Bruce Publishing Co., 1955.

Dubois, E.T. *Portrait of Leon Bloy.* New York: Sheed and Ward, 1951.

Echele, C.T., ed. *Peter Maurin: Christian Radical* St. Louis: Pio Decimo Press, 1959.

Ellis, John Tracy. *American Catholics and the Intellectual Life.* Chicago: Heritage Foundation, 1956.

Ellis, Mark. *Peter Maurin: Prophet in the Twentieth Century* New York: Paulist Press, 1981.

Finn, James. *Pacifism and Politics.* New York: Random House, 1967.

Flynn, George Q. *American Catholics and the Roosevelt Presidency.* Lexington: University of Kentucky Press, 1968.

Furfey, Paul Hanley. *Fire on Earth.*New York: MacMillan Co., 1936.

Gill, Eric. *It All Goes Together.*New York: Devin Adair, 1944.

Gleason Phillip, ed. *Contemporary Catholicism in the United States.* South Bend: University of Notre Dame Press, 1969.

_____. *Catholicism in America.* New York: Harper Row Publishers, Inc., 1970.

Goldman, Eric. *The Crucial Decade.* New York: Alfred A. Knopf, 1956.

Greeley, Andrew. *The Catholic Experience: An Interpretation of the History of American Catholicism.* New York: Image Books, 1969.

Handlin, Oscar. *Boston's Immigrants.* New York: Atheneum Press, 1974.

Harrington, Michael. *The Other America.* New York: MacMillan Press, 1962.

Hayes, Carlton. *A Generation of Materialism.* New York: Harper and row, 1941.

Herbst, Alma. *The Negro in the Slaughtering House and Packing Industry.*Bopston: Houghton Mifflin Co., 1931.

Hitchcock, James. *The Decline and Fall of Radical Catholicism.* New York: Herder and Herder, 1971.

Hofstadter, Richard. *Anti-Intellectualism in American Life.* New York: Alfred Knopf, 1963.

Huber, Ralph, ed. *Our Bishops Speak.* Milwaukee: Bruce Publishing Co., 1952.

Iverson, Robert W. *The Communists and the Schools.* New York: Harcourt Brace and Co., 1959.
186

Bibliography

Kampelman, Max *The Communist Party vs. The CIO.*New York: Frederick Praeger, Inc., 1957.

Kantowicz, Edward. *Corporation Sole: Cardinal Mundelein and Chicago Catholicism.* South Bend, University of Notre Dame Press, 1983.

Kropotkin, Peter. *Fields, Factories and Workshops.* New York: Benjamin Blom, 1968.

La Farge, John. *The Race Question and the Negro.* New York: Longmans, Green and Company, 1943.

_____. *The Catholic Viewpoint on Race Relations*New York: Hanover House, 1956.

Lally, Francis, *The Catholic Church in a Changing America.* Boston: Little Brown, 1962.

Mc Avoy, Thomas. *The Great Crisis in American Catholic History.* Chicago: Henry Regency Co., 1957.

_____. *Roman Catholicism and the American Way of Life.* South Bend: University of Notre Dame Press, 1960.

_____. *A History of the Cathooic Church in the UNited States.* South Bend: University of Notre Dame Press, 1969.

Massee, Benjamin, ed. *The Church and Social Progress.* Milwaukee: Bruce Publishing Co., 1966.

_____. *Fifty Years of the Catholic Mind.*New York: Sheed and Ward, 1965.

Maurin, Peter. *The Green Revolution.* Chicago: Catholic Worker Press, 1976.

Michel, Virgil. *The Liturgy of the Church.* New York: MacMillan, 1937.

Miller William D. *Dorothy Day, A Biography.*
San Francisco: Harper and Row, 1982.

_____. *A Harsh and Dreadful Love: Dorothy
Day and the Catholic Worker Movement.* New York:
Liveright, 1972.

Moody, John. *Fast By the Road.* New York:
MacMIllan and Co., 1946.

Mounier, Emmanuel. *A Personalist
Manifesto*New York: Longman, Green and COmpany,
1938.

Murray, John Courtney. *We Hold These
Truths.*New York: Sheed and Ward, 1960.

Newell, Barbara Wayne. *Chicago and the Labor
Movement: Metropolitan Unionism in the 1930's.*
Urbana: University of Illinois Press, 1961.

O'Brien, David. *American Catholics and
Social Reform: The New Deal Years.* New York:
Oxford Press, 1968.

_____. *The Renewal of American
Catholicism.* New York: Oxford Press, 1972.

O'Connor, Daniel. *Catholic Social Doctrine.*
Baltimore:Westminster, 1956.

Osborne, William. *The Segregated Covenant:
Race Relations and American Catholics.* New York:
Herder and Herder, 1968.

Penty, Arthur. *A Guildsman's Interpretation of History.* London: George Allen and Unwin
Ltd., 1920.

Piehl, Mel. *Breaking Bread: The Catholic
Worker and the Origin of Catholic Radicalism in
America.* Philadelphia: Temple University Press,
1982.

Bibliography

Riga, Peter. *Catholic Thought and Crisis*. Milwaukee: Bruce Publishing Co.,1962.

_____. *The Church and Revolution*. Milwaukee: Bruce Publishing Co., 1967.

Roberts, Nancy, *Dorothy Day and the Catholic Worker*. Albany: State University of New York Press, 1984.

Rossi, Peter and Dentler, Robert. *The Politics of Urban Renewal*. Glencoe: Free Press of Glencoe, 1961.

Roy, Ralph Lord. *Communism and the Churches*. New York: Harcourt, Brace and Company, 1960.

Ryan, John. *The Alleged Socialism of the Church Fathers*. St. Louis: Herder, 1913.

Schlesinger, Arthur, Jr. *A Pilgrim's Progress* Boston: Little, Brown and COmpany, 1966.

Shanabruch, Charles. *Chicago's Catholics: The Evolution of a Catholic Identity*. South Bend: University of Notre Dame Press, 1981.

Sheehan, Arthur. *Peter Maurin: Gay Believer*. Garden City: Hanover House, 1959.

Sibley, Mulford, and Jacob, Phillip E. *Conscription of Conscience: The American State and the Conscientious Objector*. Ithaca: Cornell University Press, 1952.

Spear, Alan. *Black Chicago*. Chicago: University of Chicago Press, 1967.

Stolberg, Benjamin. *The Story of the CIO*. New York: Viking Press, 1938.

Terkel, Studs. *Hard Times: An Oral History of the Great Depression*. New York: Avon Press, 1970.

Treat, Roger L. *Bishop Sheil and the CIO* . New York: Norton Publishing Company, 1951.

Tull, Charles. *Father Coughlin and the New Deal*. Syracuse: University of Syracuse Press, 1965.

Van Allen, Rodger. *The Commonweal and American Catholicism.*Philadelphia: Fortress Press, 1974.

Vidler, A.R. *A Century of Social Catholicism.*London: S.P.C.K., 1964.

Wakin, Edward, and Scheuer, Joseph. *The De-Romanization of the American Catholic Church.* New York: MacMIllan and Company, 1966.

Walsh, Raymond. *CIO*. New York: W.W. Norton and COmpany, 1937.

Wittner, Lawrence, *Rebels Against War.* New York: Columbia University Press, 1969.

Zahn, Gordon. *War Conscience and the State.* New York: Hawthorne Books, 1967.

INTERVIEWS

Cantwell, Monsignor Daniel. Chicago, Illinois. Interview, 5 June 1976*

Claver, Sister Peter. Rome, Georgia. Interview, 26 November 1976

Doebble, John. Chicago, Illinois. Interview, 15 May 1976

Bibliography

Falls, Arthur. Chicago, Illinois. Interview 19 May 1976*

Hayes, Monsignor John. 14 June 1976*

Himbaugh, Sister Cecilia. Chicago, Illinois. 15 October 1976

Marciniak, Edward. Chicago, Illinois. Interview, 31 October 1976*

O'Gara, James. Rockville Center, New York. Interview, 22, 24 June, 1976*

O'Gara Joan Smith. Rockville Center, New York. Interview, 24 June 1976.*

Paul, Marty. Boyne City, Michigan. Interview, 17 June, 1976.

Sullivan, Tom. Rockville Center, New York. Interview, 24 June, 1976*.

---

*These taped interviews have been deposited with the Catholic Worker Collection at the Marquette University Archives, Milwaukee Wisconsin.

INDEX

Alexian Brothers
  Hospital, 143-147
Alinsky, Saul 98, 106,
107
America, 13, 164, 175
American Civil
Liberties Union (ACLU),
143
American Federation of
Labor, 40, 96, 97, 100
American Jewish Com-
mittee, 79
American Jewish Con-
gress, 79
American Mercury, 138
Association of Catholic
Conscientious Objectors
(ACCO), 139-143
Association of Catholic
Trade Union (ACTU),
110-114

"Back of the Yards",
98, 105, 106,
Berdyaev, Nicholas, 43
Bittner, Van, 105, 107
Bloy, Leon, 21, 22, 23
B'nai B'rith, 79, 84
Bowers, John 45, 46,
180
Brooklyn Tablet, 81,172
Broun, Heywood, 99

Catholic Family Life,
38
Calvin, John, 18
Cantwell, Father
Daniel, 64, 111
Carlyle, Thomas, 20, 26
Carrabine, Father
Martin, 57, 165

Carrel, Alexis, 20
Carroll, Joe, 101
Cassier, Ernst, 26
Catholic Interracial
Foundation (C.I.F.), 69
Catholic Interracial
Council (CIC), 158
Catholic Labor Alliance
(CLA), 153, 155, 157,
162
Catholic Worker Move-
ment, ii iv, 14, 25,
33-37, 41-42, 54
The Catholic Worker,
14, 19, 25, 32, 35, 36,
40, 41, 42, 52, 54, 57,
62, 72-73, 160 on
organized labor, 93,
94, 113; on pacifism,
125-126, 143, 146
Catholic Youth Organi-
zation (C.Y.O.), 52,
80, 155
Chicago Catholic Worker
Movement, 34, 39, 40,
56, 60, 144; and
blacks; 71, 73, 74; and
Jews, 82; labor
organizing, 89, 91, 96-
98, 102-104, 105-109,
113, 115; pacifism,
120, 122, 124
*Chicago Catholic
Worker*, 64, 65, 74, 79,
81, 115, 122, 123, 154,
155, 157; on union
organizing, 91, 102
103, 107
Chicago Defender, 74,
179
Chicago Federation of
Labor, 109, 157
Chicago Housing Author-
ity, 72

193

Chicago Interstudent Catholic Action (CISCA), 38, 57, 80, 111, 165
Chicago Tribune, 39, 40, 59, 90, 109
Christian Family Life Movement, 87
Christian Front, 78, 79, 80, 83, 84, 85
Civilian Public Service, 139
Cogley, John, v, 35, 41, 44, 48, 52-54, 58-59, 61-62, 70-73, 80-82, 86-87, 90, 91, 93, 160, 161, 163, 164; confrontation with Coughlin, 78; and world war II, 139, 149, 151, as editor of *Commonweal*, 165-179; on the Catholic Worker, 181
Committee of Catholics Opposed to Anti-Semitism, 159
Commonweal, v, 28, 113, 123, 137, 166-173, 182
Communist Party, 892
Congress of Industrial Organization (C.I.O.) 94, 95, 97, 98, 104, 106, 108, 112, 113, 153
Cort, John, 110
Costello, Donald, 88
Coughlin, Father Charles, 77, 81
Coughlinites, 77, 81
Cowley, Malcolm, 29

Daily Worker, 84, 92
Darwin, Charles, 21

Day, Dorothy, iii, iv, 25, 27, 28, 29, 31, 34, 35, 37, 39, 41, 49 55, 57, 83, 153, 160,; on organized labor, 89 90, 96, 113; on farm commune, 115, and pacifism, 121, 123, 124-126, 137, 141, 145 post war years, 169, 175, 177-179
Dell, Floyd, 29
de Maistre, Joseph, 20
De Paul University, 64
Dilling, Elizabeth, 16
Doebble, John, 143-144
Dostoevsky, Fyodor, 18

"Easy Essays", 17, 21, 75, 118
Egan, John, 73
Ellis, Mark, 93

Falls, Arthur, 35-37, 39-42, 48, 57, 68, 69, 71-74, 89
Farmer, James, 146,
Federation News, 100, 109
Fellowship of Reconciliation, 142
Fordham University, 83
Franco, Francisco, 121
French, Paul, 141
Furfey, Paul Hanley, 4

Gavagan-Fish Anti-Lynching Bill, 73
Gavagan, Thomas, 157
Ghandi, Mahatma, i, 95 114
Girdler, Tom, 90
Gold, Mike, 30

Guild-Hearst Strike News, 101, 102, 104
Greeley, Andrew, 88
Green, William, 97,

Harrington, Michael, 176
Hayes, Carlton, 28
Hayes, Father John, 35, 41, 46, 106-107, 110-111, 124
Herald American, 102
Higgins, Monsignor George, 178
Hillenbrand, Father Reynold 52, 57, 101, 110, 111
Himbaugh, Sister Cecilia, 57
Hitler, Adolph, i
Horner, Henry, 59
Hugo, Father John, 123-124
Hyde Park Norwood Community Conference, 72

Ignatius Loyola, 22
Interracial Council, 75

Jewish Labor Committee, 78
Jones, Rufus, 140

Karlin, Terry, 30
Kropotkin, Peter, 19, 21, 22
Ku Klux Klan, 77

Labor Schools, 110-111
Leo XIII, Pope, 15
Levi, Emmanuel, 99
Lewis, John L., 108
Ligourian Fathers, 166

Loyola University of Chicago, 42, 66, 166, 167
Lucey, Bishop Robert E., 95

Mc Carthy, Frank, 108
Mc Carthy, Senator Joseph, 171-173
Mc Donald, Dwight, iii, 173, 177
Mc Kay, Claude, 75
Marciniak, Edward, vi, 37-39, 53, 56-57, 64, 73, 75 84; labor organizing, 91-93, 96-97, 105-106, 112-114, 117, 178, 179; and world war II, 120, 139, 146, 150-151;and the CLA, 153-162
Maritain, Jacques, 20, 22, 42-43
Maritain, Raissa, 22, 43
Marx, Karl, 17, 18, 21
Maurin, Peter, iii,v, 13-32, 34-36, 42, 56, 80; on labor unions, 93-96, 109, 113-114, farm commune, 114-115
Maynard, Thomas, 138,
Mennonites, 139
Meyer, Karl, 183
Michel, Father Virgil, 43, 85
Mooney, Archbishop Edward, 85
Morrison, Father Joseph, 153
Mounier, Emmanuel, 98, 21, 23, 24, 43
Mundelein, George William Cardinal, 57, 67,

120; and anti-semitism,
79; on union organiz-
ing, 98, 105-111
Murray, Phillip, 112

National Service Board
for Religious Objec-
tors, 139-140
Newman, John Cardinal,
17
Newspaper Guild, 99-102
New World, 101-103
New Yorker, iii, 177
Northwestern
University, 42
Notre Dame University,
82

O'Brien, David, iii,
77, 94, 168, 174
O'Gara, James, 47, 53,
120, 164-168, 173-174
Of Human Importance,
147
O'Neil Eugene, 30
Osborne, William, 158

Packinghouse Workers
Organizing Committee
(PWOC) 105-109, 155
Park Manor Investment
Association, 158
Parsons, Wilfrid, 13,
138
Patriotic Research
Bureau, 160
Paul, Marty, 56, 116,
179
Personalism, 24, 44
Pius XII, Pope, 81
Populism, link to
Coughlinism, 77
Preis, Art, 112

Quakers, 139

Read, Harry, 102
Republic Steel, 89, 98
Reser, Al, 56, 58, 106
173
Reser, Catherine, 115
Reuther, Walter, 44
Rinehold, Father H.A.,
125, 164-165
Roe, Walter, 148
Rogan, Jim, 144, 146
Rosenberg, Julius and
Ethel, 179
Rosenwald Foundation,
160
Ryan, Monsignor John,
94

Saint Elizabeth Church
67-68, 74-75
Saint Ignatius Church,
13
Saint Joseph House of
Hospitality, 56, 57,
58, 60, 70, 110, 144
St. Jude Messenger, 16
Saint Patrick Church,
39
Sandburg, Carl, 64
Schuster, George, 28
Seattle Catholic Worke
House, 125
Seltzer, Louis, 170
Sheehan, Arthur, 23,
140, 141
Sheil, Bishop Bernard,
53, 57; and anti-
semitism, 79; and unio
organizing, 101, 103,
105, 109
Sheil School of Social
Studies, 166

Shriver, Sargent, 158
Sign, 171
Skillin, Ed, 167
Social Justice, 79
Spanish Civil War, 121,
122
Spellman, John Car-
dinal, 172
Spillane, Mickey, 170
Steel Workers Organiz-
ing Committee, 89,
Stoddard Camp 141
Sullivan, Thomas, 46,
53, on farm commune,
116; and world war II,
137; at New York
Catholic Worker House,
173-177

Taylor Street House of
Hospitality, 47, 56, 71
Tawney, R.H., 19
Temporary Woodlawn
Organization, 159
Terkel, Studs, 61
Texaco Oil Company, 122
The Other America, 177
*Today,*165, 166

Union Square 19, 32
University of Chicago,
42, 47, 72, 83
Urban League, 36, 71

Van Allen, Rodger, 167
Vietnam War, 183
Voice, 83-84

Work, 73, 153-160, 178

Young, George, 39

Zahn, Gordon, 152